M000247849

MALIBU
FARM
Cookbook

Recipes from the California Coast

MALIBU
FARM
Cookbook

Helene Henderson

Photographs by Martin Löf

CLARKSON POTTER/PUBLISHERS

NEW YORK

Copyright © 2014 by Helene Henderson
Photographs copyright © by 2014 Martin Löf

All rights reserved.

Published in the United States by Clarkson Potter/Publishers,
an imprint of the Crown Publishing Group, a division of
Penguin Random House LLC, New York.
www.clarksonpotter.com
www.crownpublishing.com

CLARKSON POTTER and colophon are registered trademarks of
Penguin Random House LLC.

Originally published by Artimal Books, Stockholm, Sweden,
in 2014.

Library of Congress Cataloging-in-Publication Data is available.

ISBN 978-1-101-90736-8
eBook ISBN 978-1-101-90737-5

Printed in China

10 9 8 7 6 5 4

First Clarkson Potter Edition

CONTENTS

INTRODUCTION

Malibu is a small town stretched over twenty-seven miles; a town with one highway, one movie theater, and one high school, just like any other small town in America.

OK, maybe not exactly the same: Add a few surfers, epic beaches and waves, movie stars, and a perpetual California summer. But Malibu is more than beaches and surfing. There is the hidden Malibu, which most day visitors and tourists never encounter.

In the backyards here, chickens and organic vegetable gardens are as common as surfboards and golf carts. (A golf cart is a necessity for heading to the beach.) Vineyards small and large dot the hillsides. Hobby winemakers, movie star winemakers, and large-scale wine-making operations are beginning to challenge the more well-known wines from Napa and the central coast of California. Having your own fruit orchards or olive oil production is a pretty standard backyard practice. Having a beehive is Malibu bee-havior.

Whether a bum or a billionaire, everyone in Malibu dresses the same, which means no jackets, no ties. A Malibu "suit" is a wet suit, a bathing suit, or a bee suit.

I did not grow up in Malibu. I did not even grow up in America. I was born in Luleå, in the very north of Sweden, near the Finnish border—pretty much as far away from Malibu as you can get. I came to America as so many immigrants before me, with a one-way ticket, $500, and a heart full of the American dream. I knew nobody when I stepped off the plane, and I barely spoke English.

My father was an African American jazz musician, who met my mother while touring in Sweden. Although he left my mother behind to raise me without assistance or financial support, I did hold the "golden ticket": an American passport, acquired at birth.

Because my mother worked in restaurants as a waitress, so did I, starting at a very young age. Soon I transitioned out of waitressing and began to work in a restaurant kitchen. I learned cooking first from my mother and then from cooks in small, nonglamorous kitchens in Sweden. Cooking was not fashionable or even considered a career for women at the time. When I left for America, I left to find bigger and better things. I modeled and worked as a graphic designer, but somehow the kitchen always drew me back in.

I met my husband John some years later. He is a surfer and wanted to be near the beach, and I was looking for land where I could have a few vegetable beds. We moved to Malibu in 2008, after a long search for the perfect house. We finally found our little neglected Craftsman house on a two-acre lot filled with weeds and potential. There were also a rusty old barn and a corral. Our neighbor had horses and twenty-eight very loud peacocks.

The fight for the land began right after we moved in. It was us against the weeds. Sad to say, weeding on the hillside gave me a bad case of poison oak: round one to the weeds. But while I recovered, I thought of a brilliant solution. Instead of weeding the yard myself, I would get goats to clear the land. We already had a barn and a corral, and goats on Craigslist were less than $40—and so with a few computer strokes, we had farm animals.

The solution was not as brilliant as I had first thought. The goats turned out to be very picky eaters—they knew they were residents of Malibu from the day they arrived and smelled the ocean breeze. They simply refused to eat the weeds that were all around them. They preferred alfalfa, roses, or fruit trees. They loved walks on the beach. In Malibu, everyone turns out to be a beach bum sooner rather than later, even Nubian/Boer mix goats. We were back to square one and ended up clearing the weeds by hand while the goats watched from nearby.

Our daughter, Celia, started college on the East Coast that year and wanted a pig. And we were the parents who

thought that it was a perfectly reasonable request from a child no longer living at home, and so that year Santa brought a potbellied pig for Christmas. The pig would become the best friend of our son Casper. In his junior year of high school, the pig was his prom date. They wore matching bow ties, rode in a limousine together to a Beverly Hills hotel, and lasted about 45 minutes in the ballroom before hotel security escorted them out. It made his school's "best of" list for 2010: Casper and his pig date.

Once you have goats, a pig, dogs, and a cat, chickens and bees are bound to follow. We planted a vineyard, fruit trees, and vegetable gardens, and Malibu Farm, our backyard, was complete.

I had previously worked in catering for many years, and when we moved to Malibu I went into private chef work. A private chef is someone who goes to the client's home, usually someone very rich, and makes dinner for the family. I called myself a "cooler lady." Not someone "cool," but someone who brings a cooler to work. At the request of a few local moms, I started teaching cooking classes during the day from my home while still working as a private chef at night. I began a blog as a place to post recipes for my students—and Malibu Farm the blog was born.

My classes were great fun. We picked produce in the yard, and then we cooked up a big lunch as part of the lesson. After a year of classes, the participants suggested I throw a dinner party so that the husbands could join the fun. I wasn't sure that anyone would pay admission to attend a dinner party in my backyard, so I turned it into a fundraiser for Point Dume Marine Science Elementary School. I asked other local producers to join me: Sonja Magdevski, who lives two blocks away from me and produces Casa Dumetz Wines; Robert Jaye from Malibu Olive Company; Bruce Lampcov from Malibu Honey; Doug Burdge and his colleagues from Malibu Mary; Danette McReynolds from Chèvre Lavande; and Lawrence Charles of Charles & Company, which sells organic and kosher teas.

I thought of that dinner as a one-time event, but immediately everyone was asking when the next one would be, and so they became a monthly event. Guests would be presented with a "treasure map" when they arrived, guiding them around the property:

In the front yard, meet the furry-footed hens and Arnold the pig—eat deviled eggs with bacon.

In the vegetable garden, eat freshly picked crudités.

By the barn, meet Casey and Quincy the goats—eat goat cheese pizza.

In the vineyard, meet Sonja—have a glass of Pinot.

By the beehives, meet Bruce—sample cheese and honey.

Then meet us at the long table for a family-style meal.

Casper's jazz band provided the music, and his friends were the servers. After a few events, the guests were no longer just local friends. People from San Diego, New York, and Arizona were buying tickets and attending my farm dinners. Celebrities followed: Pink, Jakob Dylan, Beck, Pamela Anderson, Rick Rubin, Patrick Dempsey, Ron and Kelly Meyer, and Tori Spelling. Despite all this, Malibu Farm was still very much a backyard operation. Sometimes I wondered whether anyone would notice that it wasn't really a farm—it was just a two-acre backyard with farm animals; we grew what we could eat, and we did not grow food commercially—but nobody questioned the name and everybody loved the "farm." And then I realized that it was the accessibility of the place that was so appealing. Nothing here was perfect, but it was perfectly imperfectly inspiring.

My farm is a farm you could have too. Maybe it would be smaller, but even a small city yard can have a few vegetable beds, a small hive, or a couple of chickens. My vegetable beds are built out of scrap wood, the chicken coop is a trellis enclosed with chicken wire, and the pig lives in an old doghouse. Malibu Farm is my home. I came here with nothing and ended up with everything.

My mother lived in my childhood home in Sweden until she passed away in the spring of 2012. One of the last things my mother said to me was that she hoped that I would not lose touch with Sweden—that I would stay connected to my homeland and not forget my mother tongue. But on my flight back home to Los Angeles after her funeral, I doubted I would ever return. And then Martin came calling.

Word of the lure of the "Malibu farm" had somehow crossed the Atlantic and reached the gifted Martin Löf, a lifestyle photographer from Sweden. I received an email request from him, asking if he could photograph my next backyard farm dinner. At first I thought, *Who is this Martin?* And my natural reaction would have been to say no, but then I thought of my mother, and I decided to say yes to Sweden and yes to Martin.

Martin came and took some photos, and I didn't think much about it until I saw the photos. And I was totally blown away. I knew my mother had sent me a gift from Sweden. Martin was in love with Malibu and wanted to return to work on a book together—and so he did, and here is our collaboration.

The photos in this book were shot over a few days. Every dish in this book is real. Nothing was fussed over or made as "food photography." All the dishes we photographed were made for catering jobs, to fulfill private chef commitments, or as part of Malibu Farm dinners. Every photo in this book is of a dish somebody ate. And every dish in this book looks spectacular because of the talents of Martin Löf.

During the production of this book, an opportunity presented itself. I was offered a short-term pop-up restaurant on the Malibu Pier, which turned into a long-term lease. In one year, I went from being a "cooler lady" running a backyard, underground operation to being the owner of a bustling café with forty employees. I am often asked how I thought of the idea of the café (also called Malibu Farm). Some wonder why I decided to not serve soft drinks or French fries, the usual staples of a casual café located on a pier. The answer of course is, Wherever I go, I will always be me. I cook what I cook, wherever I am. At the café, we serve the same dishes we cooked in my classes and served at the farm dinners.

I did not start Malibu Farm the blog or even Malibu Farm the café by myself. But it is all the ultimate proof that if you do what comes naturally, stay true to yourself, and have the support of your community, anything is possible.

Malibu Farm is a home, a community, and a desire to live local, eat local, and celebrate local. Obviously, the food is organic. The wheat is almost always whole wheat. Lots of veggies and whole grains.

Here in the 'Bu, we raise free-range, fancy, feather-footed chickens who all have names. We still eat chicken, just really super small portions of it. OK, we have a pig too, who is super cute, super hungry, super fat. But shh, don't tell Arnold that we still eat pork. Prosciutto, bacon, salami—that stuff is just too delicious to give up. I don't have any cows, and I don't eat red meat. But once in a blue moon, here on the farm we grill a steak for our guests. I grew up fishing and love seafood, but let's not deplete our treasures from the sea. Our portions are small and of sustainable seafood only.

Nothing low-fat or nonfat, 'cause nothing makes you fatter than eating fat-free. This is a fact. Eat the real thing or don't eat it at all. No fake food. Margarine, vegan butter, artificial sweeteners? What is that stuff? If you don't know how to make it or where it comes from, don't eat it. Don't buy it.

Malibu Farm Cookbook is your guide to the Malibu I live in and the Malibu I love. The Malibu where goats are beach bums, and where the cackle of chickens and the low buzzing of bees accompany the sound of crashing waves.

The recipes in this book are tried and true, and super easy to make. A few notes on how I cook—take these, leave them, or adapt them to your own tastes and preferences.

Recipe for Malibu Farm

1 Swedish chef
2 spoiled goats
1 fat pig
23 fancy-footed chickens
2 rescue dogs
1 daring outdoor cat named Fennel
1 queen bee + her colony of
    worker bees
1 small vineyard
300 raspberry bushes
36 fruit trees
12 vegetable beds
28 loud peacocks
the most beautiful beach

I cook primarily with extra-virgin olive oil. Sometimes I use an unflavored vegetable oil. I love butter but butter burns very easily, so when I sauté, I add olive oil to the butter to raise the smoke point.

For many recipes, I do not include a measurement for salt. To become an expert at properly seasoning your foods, choose one unrefined salt (such as gray Celtic sea salt or pink Himalayan salt) and use it all the time. Different unrefined salts have a totally different flavor and saltiness, so switching from one to another is going to change how much salt you need. It is usually easier to work with a medium coarse salt than a super fine salt. Aim for a very even but light salt distribution. Start with less and add more if needed.

I don't like black pepper very much and so I use it only occasionally.

Don't crowd your pan—cook fewer items, in several batches.

Everything tastes better with something acidic added. A splash of vinegar or lemon will elevate any dish.

This cookbook is not your usual collection of breakfast, sides, and all that. I arranged these recipes just how I would a treasure map for a dinner guest at my home. You'll move around the grounds, with each chapter highlighting something special that you might find around the next corner. So come on in, enjoy the views, and have something great to eat. Welcome to Malibu Farm.

FROM
THE COOP

I have always had chickens. Even when we lived in Los Angeles and had only a small city plot, we had backyard chickens. Having a backyard coop is super easy. All you need to provide is shelter, fresh water, and feed.

Every time I come home, the chickens come running to greet me. It never gets old and always puts a smile on my face. They come in anticipation of treats, of course, and there is no easier way to compost your vegetable scraps. And in return you get the most glorious eggs every day, a gift that keeps on giving. If you have chickens, you will always have something to eat.

A lot of brands sell eggs laid by chickens that have been fed a vegetarian diet, which does not make any sense. Chickens by nature are not vegetarian—they love worms, bugs, and any scraps they can find, not necessarily vegetarian. Although we feed our chickens, they graze on our property and could probably survive just on what they find around the yard. We have had to fence off many of the vegetable beds, because otherwise they find their way into them all the time. Except arugula—no critters or chickens or goats eat it, and that makes it one of the easiest crops to grow organically.

And OK, even though I love chickens, I sometimes eat chicken, although never my own chickens—except that one time when we wanted to take self-sufficiency to the next level. The free-range birds were tasty but very lean. The whole experience turned my younger son, Caden, vegan, which he still is. So proceed with caution if you have young children and plan to eat your own flock.

My friend Chris Cortazzo, a Malibu realtor, has the most gorgeous wild turkeys on his oceanfront estate (p. 251).

FRITTATA WITH RICOTTA AND PEAS

8 eggs

1 teaspoon salt

¼ cup heavy cream or milk

1 cup ricotta cheese

⅓ cup three-cheese
  blend, shredded

1 cup frozen peas

1 cup cherry tomatoes,
  halved

1 cup sliced button
  mushrooms, sautéed
  for 5 minutes in a hot
  skillet until browned

¼ cup grated Parmesan
  cheese

Frittata is an egg-cellent breakfast dish, especially for large groups. So much faster to make than omelets!

Stir together eggs with loads of cheese; add vegetables; and slide the whole thing into the oven. Good morning!

Whisk together eggs and salt in a bowl; add cream, ricotta cheese, and shredded cheese. Stir to combine, but keep ricotta cheese lumpy. Stir in frozen peas, cherry tomatoes, and sautéed mushrooms. Pour into small individual cast-iron skillets or into an 8-inch round cake pan.

Dust the grated Parmesan cheese over the frittatas, and bake in a preheated 400 degree oven until cooked through—about 12 minutes for individual frittatas and up to 40 minutes for a large frittata.

If using a round cake pan, invert it to turn the frittata out of the pan. Then turn the frittata over and cut into slices.

Serve warm or at room temperature.

Tip: To more easily turn the frittata out of the pan, line the bottom of the pan with parchment paper and grease the sides before pouring in the egg mixture.

FRIED EGG SANDWICHES

Makes 2 sandwiches

4 eggs
Butter
Olive oil
2 slices Havarti cheese
Lemon aioli: add grated
   garlic and a squeeze of
   lemon juice to mayo
4 slices of good crusty
   bread, toasted just
   before using
Small bunch of arugula
4 slices bacon, cooked
   until fat rendered and
   drained on paper towels

I love a fried egg sandwich in the morning. Or, enjoyed with a beer, it could be a late lunch. Sometimes it's even better for a late-night dinner.

Assemble your ingredients. Then fry the eggs, two at a time, in a dab of butter and a little olive oil, until crispy around the edges—cooked as much or as little as you wish. Sunny-side up or flip it over. Top with slice of cheese.

Give them a dash of salt, then remove to a plate and cook the other two eggs.

Put the sandwiches together: slather aioli on each bottom slice of bread, top with arugula, add two cooked eggs each and crispy bacon. Finish with the top slices of bread, also slathered with aioli.

SMOKED SALMON–
RICOTTA SCRAMBLE

Makes 4 to 6 servings

8 eggs
½ cup ricotta cheese
    or crème fraîche
Olive oil or butter
8 slices smoked salmon
    or gravlax, chopped
2 tablespoons fresh
    herbs, chopped

As a family, we very seldom have a sit-down breakfast. Actually, we have it only twice a year: on Christmas Eve and on Christmas Day. It's a tradition here on the farm.

For Christmas Eve we have Swedish mini-pancakes with cream and berries (p. 37), and for Christmas Day we have smoked salmon–ricotta scramble, and either broccoli mashed potatoes (p. 71) or crispy parsnip-potato latkes (p. 179).

I also love something spicy with eggs— try them with Lazy Woman's Salsa (p. 65).

In a medium bowl, beat the eggs with the ricotta cheese or crème fraîche and a sprinkle of salt.

Heat some olive oil or butter in a medium-size skillet, and soft scramble the eggs by gently whisking the mixture around. Add the smoked salmon or gravlax when the eggs are almost done.

Stir in some herbs and serve.

MULTIGRAIN
YOGURT PANCAKES

Makes 10 pancakes

For batter:
¼ cup dry nine-grain hot
  cereal mix, softened in
  water for 30 minutes
10 tablespoons
  all-purpose flour
1 tablespoon sugar
1 teaspoon baking soda
¼ teaspoon salt
1 cup yogurt
2 large eggs
½ teaspoon vanilla

For cooking:
Butter and olive oil

For serving:
Maple syrup
Additional butter
Crispy bacon bits
Fresh fruit

I am not a huge fan of pancakes, but I *love* this multigrain version. The batter will last for twenty-four hours, so you can make it the day before, and all you'll have to do is cook them up in the morning.

I usually keep my bacon in the freezer, which allows me to thinly slice it when needed. I fry up some thin slivers to garnish the pancakes. Super delish.

Drain the presoaked hot cereal mix and stir together with the remaining batter ingredients.

Cook the pancakes in preheated skillet in a little butter and olive oil. Flip when bubbles appear on the surface of the pancake, and cook on the opposite side until cooked through.

Drizzle with maple syrup. Top with butter, bacon bits, fresh fruit, or any combination you like.

SWEDISH MINI-PANCAKES WITH CREAM AND BERRIES

<u>Makes 4 servings</u>

For batter:
3 eggs
1 cup all-purpose flour
1 tablespoon sugar
1½ cups milk
3 tablespoons butter,
  melted

For cooking:
Additional butter

For serving:
Berries
Whipped cream

I love making mini-pancakes by using a special pan that makes seven dollar-sized pancakes at once, which is what we do at the café. When we first opened the café, we spent about thirty minutes a day making pancakes, and then we increased the time to one hour. Now, one person makes Swedish pancakes about fourteen hours a week—and we still sell out some days.

These pancakes freeze really well. For my family for Christmas Eve, I always make and freeze them ahead of time, so all we have to do in the morning is reheat and serve.

Blend all the batter ingredients together in a food processor or blender, or whisk them together in a large bowl. Then heat a mini-pancake skillet if you have one (otherwise use a cast-iron skillet or a nonstick pan), and brush with butter.

Pour a very thin layer of batter into the pan, and then lift and tilt the pan so that the batter covers most of the surface. The thinner the pancake, the better. When the edges begin to brown (in about 30 seconds), flip the pancake to cook the other side.

Once done, remove the pancake and slide it onto a plate to keep warm. Continue on with additional pancakes until the batter is gone.

Serve with berries and whipped cream.

QUINOA-OATMEAL CEREAL

Makes 8 servings

For cereal:
1 cup well-rinsed quinoa
    (some brands are
    prerinsed; check box)
1 cup old-fashioned oats,
    gluten free or regular
1 teaspoon salt

For serving:
Coconut milk
Maple syrup
Fresh or dried berries
Nuts

This recipe does not have any eggs, so it is not "from the coop." But it is a great protein-packed vegan breakfast dish. Gluten-free oats work well.

You can use any quinoa/oatmeal percentage combination; the recipe that follows is a 50/50 blend. The cereal will last several days in the fridge. Just reheat in the microwave, or stir in a small pan on the stove for a few minutes until heated.

Combine quinoa, oats, and salt with 8 cups water, and simmer for 20 minutes or until the cereal is a soft, welcoming morning mash.

Serve with coconut milk, maple syrup, fresh or dried berries, nuts, or any combination you like.

COCONUT GRANOLA

Makes 6 to 8 servings

2 cups oats

1 cup walnuts

½ cup raw pumpkin seeds

2 tablespoons sesame
seeds

3 tablespoons brown rice
syrup

3 tablespoons coconut
oil, melted

Flaked, sweetened
coconut

½ cup dried berries,
such as cherries,
cranberries, or both

We usually serve Malibu granola at the café. It's nicknamed The Mayor's Granola because Laura Rosenthal, who served as the mayor of Malibu, makes it.

She will not share her super secret recipe, but making your own version is easy. I prefer it full of nuts and dried berries, but you can mix almost anything into it.

This recipe is vegan and gluten free. I usually eat my granola with unflavored kefir, but if you serve it with almond milk, it will remain vegan.

Combine the oats, walnuts, pumpkin seeds, and sesame seeds in a medium-sized bowl. Toss with the brown rice syrup and coconut oil. Season with salt.

Place on a baking sheet, and bake in a preheated 375 degree oven for 15 to 20 minutes, stirring occasionally, until the ingredients start to toast. Then add the sweetened coconut and the dried berries, and return to the oven for 5 more minutes.

Transfer the granola to a plate and let it cool. It will crisp as it cools.

GARDEN LOVE SMOOTHIE

Serves 4 kids or 2 adults

2 cups frozen fruit (or
  fresh from the garden!)
2 cups hemp mylk
  (or 2 cups filtered water
  and 2 tablespoons hemp
  seeds and a date)
¼ cup leaves: spinach,
  collards, kale,
  nettles, stevia, grape,
  goji berry, raspberry,
  and/or passion fruit
  leaves (or a variety
  of edible leaves from
  the garden) . . . stems
  mostly removed
1 tablespoon bee pollen
1 tablespoon goji berries

Start your day with a bang! This recipe comes from June Louks, who wrote a *Malibu Mom's Manifesto on Fresh Whole Food*.

The night before: De-seed and cut up fruit (10 strawberries with two bananas is the Louks girls' favorite combination). Put it in a freezer bag, and freeze.

In the morning: Put fruit, mylk, and leaves in the blender and blend. If you are a fresh food kid, blend only if your parents have shown you how. How long? It depends on your blender. Pour into glasses and sprinkle with bee pollen and goji berries. Voilà!

Tip: Fresh goji berries grow like weeds here in Malibu!

MALIBU FARM
DEVILED EGGS

Makes 12 servings

12 eggs
½ cup sriracha mayo
   (p. 242)
6 bacon strips, cooked
¼ cup arugula, julienned

Three things make hard-boiled eggs easier to peel:

1. Don't use a super fresh egg (those are *impossible* to peel).
2. Always start your eggs in cold water.
3. Always finish your eggs in ice-cold water.

I don't care for the yolk that much, so often I use quail eggs when making deviled eggs. A small deviled egg goes a long way in my book.

Add the eggs to a pan and cover with cold water. Place over high heat and bring the water to a boil, then turn off the heat. Cover and let sit for 12 minutes. Transfer to ice-cold water and allow to cool before peeling.

Cut the cooled, peeled hard-boiled eggs in half crosswise. Then cut off the tip ends to make it stand up without rolling over. Have them as a snack, or add them to a bowl and make a single serving of egg salad for later.

Remove the yolks entirely, and add a nice dollop of sriracha mayo to the egg white. Then return a small piece of yolk on top of the mayo, and top with crumbled cooked bacon and some julienned arugula. Allow 1 egg (2 deviled egg pieces) per person.

FROM THE FARM

and the vegetable beds

When we first moved to Malibu, I set out to plant only things that we could eat or that were native or water-wise plants. Our property is on a hill. The house is on top, where it's flat, and that's where we put our vegetables beds, built out of scrap wood. On the first slope we planted three hundred vine grapes (Malbec and Carmenere). Then there is another flat area, where the barn and corral are, and that's where we planted three hundred raspberry bushes.

Down below the barn area and near the creek bed that leads to the beach, there was already a fruit orchard with about forty trees, most of them surrounded by weeds. We cleared and cleaned and planted about thirty-five more trees. Malibu has a great climate for growing almost everything year-round.

Larry Thorne grows the most amazing strawberries in the heart of Malibu. You have not had strawberries until you have had his. His family has been farming in Malibu for more than sixty years, and they produce an incredible crop of strawberries, tomatoes, kale, corn, zucchini, heirloom tomatoes, watermelons, oranges, and basil. A lot of it is grown by dry farming, using only the year's rainfall to produce a crop. When we first opened the café, he donated a large crop of watermelons and oranges, which inspired us to make fresh-squeezed juices, now a very popular item on the menu.

Alice Bamford and One Gun Ranch also grow amazing local produce. They specialize in lettuces, arugula, carrots, and chard. They make their own organic compost. Both the produce and the compost are available at local farmers markets. The sweetness of their produce is credited to their premium growing medium.

Mike Gardner (p. 158/163) is a successful realtor, an awesome photographer, a fisherman, a forager, and a hunter. He also has the most incredible backyard farm. His produce is not available commercially, but we use it for our events all the time (p. 46/47).

KALE CAESAR

Makes 4 servings

For dressing:
2 tablespoons mayonnaise
2 tablespoons grated
 Parmesan cheese
1 lemon, juiced
Splash of Worcestershire
 sauce
1 garlic clove, grated
Pinch of salt
¼ cup olive oil

For salad:
1 bunch black kale, cut
 or ripped into medium-
 size pieces; toss with
 salt and olive oil, and
 massage gently until
 leaves are glossy
Small handful sage
 leaves; fry in olive oil
 for a few seconds until
 crispy, drain on paper
 towels, and sprinkle
 with salt
½ head iceberg or
 romaine lettuce, sliced

For garnish:
Croutons
Watermelon radish

You can never go wrong with the Kale Caesar. This recipe calls for half iceberg or romaine lettuce, but you can do all kale if you wish.

I love how the sage leaves are exactly the color of the kale. Their crunchy bite mixed into the salad is a nice surprise.

At the café, we sometimes forgo the traditional croutons and top the salad with a sliced watermelon radish instead—it's more popular that way—but you decide what you like!

Whisk together all the dressing ingredients in a large bowl. Toss the salad ingredients with the dressing.

Garnish with croutons smashed into fine bread crumbs or with thinly sliced watermelon radish.

BABY POTATOES
+ GREEN BEANS

Makes 4 servings

½ pound baby potatoes
¼ cup olive oil
1 garlic clove
2 tablespoons chopped
   parsley
½ pound thin green beans
   or asparagus

I love baby potatoes and could eat them every day, at every meal. I may be a Malibu farmer now, surrounded by people who fear starch, but I'm still a Swede.

When it comes to the baby potato, smaller is better, and a fingerling is best, always with the skin on.

Boil potatoes in salted water until just done (5 to 10 minutes, depending on the size). Drain and dry.

Toss with 2 tablespoons olive oil, garlic, and parsley, and transfer to a skillet. Sauté for a few minutes, until the potatoes just begin to brown. Remove and season with salt.

Meanwhile, cook the green beans in salted water for 1 minute—undercooking is always OK but overcooking is totally gross, so when in doubt, pull them out! Toss with the remaining 2 tablespoons olive oil and a sprinkle of salt, and combine the potatoes with the green beans. Serve hot or at room temperature.

Tip: These go well on a tray of crudités with black olive dip (p. 210).

SAFFRON ISRAELI COUSCOUS WITH CORN AND SUGAR SNAP PEAS

Makes 6 servings

1 box Israeli couscous
6 cups chicken stock, vegetable stock, or water
Pinch of saffron
3 ears of super fresh sweet corn kernels, sliced from the cob
2 tablespoons butter
¼ cup olive oil
1 garlic clove, grated
Juice and zest of 1 lemon
2 cups sugar snap peas, flash blanched and sliced thin
1 bunch parsley, chopped

I love cooking with tone-on-tone colors. Coloring the Israeli couscous with saffron makes it fragrant and beautifully yellow; it looks exactly like corn kernels, and when mixed with sweet corn, you can't tell them apart. Such fun!

Cook the Israeli couscous in stock or water and a pinch of saffron, per the package instructions. (If the couscous you bought came with a seasoning packet, throw it away.)

Cook the corn in the butter and 1 tablespoon of olive oil for a few minutes, until it is just beginning to brown. Season to taste with salt and pepper.

Transfer the couscous to a bowl, season with 3 tablespoons of olive oil, garlic, lemon juice and zest, and additional salt and pepper. Stir in the cooked corn, blanched sugar snap peas, and parsley. Taste for seasoning and add more lemon juice if needed, because there is no such thing as too much lemon.

Serve hot or at room temperature.

PEA AND PESTO COUSCOUS

1 cup Israeli couscous,
  cooked in stock,
  preferably chicken,
  until just done
Lots of fresh or frozen
  peas, tossed into the
  cooking couscous just
  before draining
Splash of good olive oil
½ cup or so of pesto
  (homemade or
  purchased) to taste
1 lemon, juiced
1 garlic clove, grated
Lots of chopped parsley

Optional:
Thinly sliced, flash-
  cooked asparagus
Green beans
Sugar snap peas

Sometimes I make the saffron Israeli couscous with corn and sugar snap peas (p. 59), which I love, and other times I make this pea and pesto couscous. Either is a great side dish, combining 50 percent vegetable (either corn or peas) with the grain, which really lightens up the dish.

This is super fast if you use frozen peas and purchased pesto. Serve with a piece of grilled chicken and a salad.

All right, you've cooked your couscous and combined it with the peas. Toss with some olive oil and salt.

Then add pesto, lemon juice, and garlic. Stir in a bunch of parsley until the dish is peas-fully green. If you wish, stir in asparagus, green beans, sugar snap peas, or some combination of these vegetables.

GREEN BEANS
+ BEETS

Green beans, lightly
  cooked until they are
  just done and still
  have a crunch
Splash of good olive oil
Kosher salt
Roasted beets (p. 266),
  cut into wedges
Small handful of seeds,
  nuts, or herbs

I am a big fan of vegetable duos. Green beans in particular can combine with almost anything! Beans with beets, corn, sweet potatoes, cherry tomatoes, or olives—the combinations are endless!

Toss the green beans with olive oil and salt to taste.

Place on a platter and garnish with beets all around. Top with seeds, nuts, or herbs.

Tip: Beets go very well with horseradish crème fraîche (p. 138). Drizzle some on top.

BROCCIMOLE

AKA BROCCOLI GUACAMOLE

Makes 1½ cups

1 cup broccoli florets
¼ cup finely chopped
   yellow onion
Jalapeño pepper, diced,
   to taste
½ bunch cilantro
2 limes, juiced

Guacamole needs no improvement. It is perfection as is—except sometimes we just want to shake things up.

Cook broccoli florets in salted water for 1 minute. Drain and combine all ingredients in a food processor, and pulse until a mash forms. Season to taste with salt. Grab a bowl of chips and dip away.

Tip: To make the broccimole creamier, add 2 ripe avocadoes.

LAZY WOMAN'S SALSA

Makes 3 cups

2 large tomatoes, chopped
   into large chunks
¼ cup chopped red onion
½ cup fresh cilantro
   leaves
1 tablespoon, or to
   taste, canned chipotle
   chili in adobo sauce
2 tablespoons fresh lime
   juice
2 teaspoons salt

The best and fastest homemade salsa.

Toss everything in a blender to combine.

RAW BRUSSELS SPROUTS WITH ALMONDS AND GRAINY MUSTARD

Makes 6 servings

2 tablespoons whole-
    grain mustard
1 lemon, juiced
4 tablespoons olive oil
1 garlic clove, grated
8 large Brussels sprouts,
    sliced super thin on
    a mandoline
½ cup chopped parsley
½ cup toasted, sliced
    almonds

Raw Brussels sprouts are super delicious and so simple to make. I toss them with the dressing just a few minutes before eating, but the thinly shaved Brussels sprouts will last for several days, so I usually slice up a large amount and have this dish for a week.

I find that some who claim to hate Brussels sprouts love them raw, so even if you don't normally like them, give this dish a chance.

The larger the sprout, the easier it is to slice it. You are going to need a mandoline for this.

Combine mustard, lemon juice, olive oil, and garlic in a bowl.
Season sliced Brussels sprouts with salt, and toss with the dressing. The sprouts should not be dry; if they are, add some more olive oil or another squeeze of lemon juice. Toss in the chopped parsley and toasted, sliced almonds.

BROCCOLI
MASHED POTATOES

These broccoli mashed potatoes are a stroke of genius. During my years in private chef work, I often cooked for families with children. The kids of course would want white rice and mashed potatoes, and the parents would want the kids to eat healthier—more whole grains and more green vegetables. One day, I came up with the broccoli mash. Kids love it and it is a staple at the café. Because the café is on the pier, diners—especially tourists—expect French fries and soft drinks, to which we reply, "We have broccoli mash and kale-apple juice."

I have served this to lots and lots of kids, and many kids who "don't eat vegetables" will eat the green mashed potatoes. It is delicious. Try it. I promise you'll like it.

recipe continues

3 large russet potatoes,
    peeled and chopped
1 stick butter—yeah,
    yeah, cry me a river
    (the more butter, the
    better the mash)
1 cup heavy cream
Broccoli, roughly the
    same amount as the
    potatoes, chopped

Cook your potatoes in boiling, salted water until just soft. Use at least 1 tablespoon salt in the water, otherwise, the potatoes will taste really bland, and you will need to add twice the salt later on.

Drain, and repeat after me the mantra of Mashed Potatoes 101: "Dry your mash or it will taste like trash." Return the drained potatoes to the hot pan, and stir over heat until the liquid has evaporated. This step is key. Then push the potatoes through a ricer and into a standing mixer. With the whisk attachment, blend in the stick of butter and ½ cup of the cream; season to taste with salt and pepper.

Blanch, boil, or steam your broccoli until just done and still bright green. Drain and place in a food processor, along with the remaining ½ cup cream, until finely chopped.

Stir the broccoli and the potatoes together, and season to taste with salt and pepper.

Tip: Never use a food processor or blender for mashed potatoes, because the texture will be horrible. We want a light, fluffy mash.

BLACK AND WHITE RICE
+ GREEN BEANS

Makes 6 to 8 servings

2 tablespoons toasted
  sesame oil
2 garlic cloves, grated
2 green onions, sliced
  thin
1 cup cooked black rice
  (you can substitute
  wild rice)
2 cups cooked white rice
Zest and juice of 1 lemon

For garnish:

1 cup cherry tomatoes,
  halved
1 cup thinly cut green
  beans (1 cup diced
  asparagus, blanched,
  would be fine too)
2 tablespoons chopped
  herbs
1 tablespoon olive oil
1 tablespoon balsamic
  vinegar
1 tablespoon toasted
  sesame seeds

I love black rice—it's so seriously nutty and super delish. At home, I usually just eat the black rice in its own simple glory, but in restaurants, I usually see it blended with another grain.

If you like black rice, try cooking it in chicken stock and eating it just the way it is. No bells, no whistles. If that's not for you, make a 40/60 blend with either farro or white rice.

Heat sesame oil in a large skillet, then cook 1 grated garlic clove and green onions for 2 minutes, or just until translucent. Add black rice and white rice. Sauté until crispy and hot. Season with salt, pepper, lemon juice and zest.

Meanwhile, make the garnish. In a small bowl, toss together tomatoes, green beans, reserved garlic clove, and herbs. Season with salt and pepper. Stir in olive oil and balsamic vinegar. Top with sesame seeds.

Toss the garnish into the hot rice. Serve hot or at room temperature.

Tip: If your skillet is not that big, cook the rice in two batches.

CHARRED BROCCOLI

+ ROSEMARY AIOLI

Makes 6 to 8 servings

2 heads of broccoli
3/4 cup mayonnaise
 (homemade or
 purchased)
3 tablespoons olive oil
1/4 cup lemon juice
2 tablespoons fresh
 rosemary, chopped

You can grill or broil broccoli just as is, but it tends to get a burned flavor, which is unpleasant. Mayonnaise has a really high smoke point and is great to grill or broil with. All the mayonnaise will burn off in the process, so you will not even know it was there, but it will protect the broccoli from tasting burned.

Relax. Please don't freak out . . . we are going to use mayo! I love the stuff. And you've heard me say it—nothing makes you fatter than eating fat-free.

Mayo can play with fire. Smear it, don't fear it, on the outside of grilled cheese sandwiches. The mayo gives it a nice golden hue.

This trick also works great for cauliflower, asparagus, or grilled green beans.

Did you think this was a recipe? Sorry!

All you need to do is toss your vegetable of choice with mayo and a little olive oil. Broil or grill your vegetable until it is charred all over, sprinkle with salt, and add a squeeze of lemon and fresh rosemary.

FARM CHICKPEA HUMMUS

For tahini:
3 tablespoons toasted
   sesame seeds
2 tablespoons olive oil
1 teaspoon sesame oil
2 tablespoons water
1 teaspoon salt

For hummus:
1 can garbanzo beans,
   rinsed and drained
1 garlic clove, grated
1 lemon, juiced

For garnish:
Olive oil
Paprika
Green herbs

You can buy hummus, of course; it is everywhere. But it takes just a few minutes to make your own—and it is so much better! I know some people who actually peel their garbanzo beans (aka chickpeas) for the smoothest possible texture. Well, that is simply ridiculous. Not only am I not going to peel my beans, I am going to keep the hummus chunky!

Add tahini ingredients to blender. If you have a high-speed blender, this would be preferable. I don't, so into a standard blender it goes—whirl, whirl—and call it a day; the tahini is gonna be chunky and imperfect.

Now add garbanzo beans, garlic, and lemon juice. Season to taste with salt and pepper. Blend, blend, whirl, whirl.

If it's too thick, thin with water, additional olive oil, or both. If necessary, season with additional salt, pepper, and lemon juice.

If you like, garnish with additional olive oil, paprika, and green herb of choice. (In the winter, I garnish with pomegranate seeds.)

SMOKED
EGGPLANT DIP

1 large eggplant

1/2 medium yellow onion,
  chopped

2 tablespoons olive oil

1 tablespoon yellow
  mustard seeds

2 large, ripe tomatoes,
  chopped

2 limes, juiced

1 garlic clove, grated

1/2 cup chopped cilantro

Eggplant soaks up a lot of oil, so here is a recipe that uses none during the cooking process.

This recipe generates a lot of smoke, which gives the eggplant a great flavor. If you don't like your kitchen getting all smoked up, you can make it on a covered barbecue grill.

I love the addition of yellow mustard seeds here, which look very similar to the eggplant seeds.

Place the eggplant in a dry cast-iron skillet or on a grill on high heat. Keep covered. Turn the eggplant every few minutes until it collapses (about 20 minutes). Poke to check for softness. It is going to get smoky!

Meanwhile, sauté the onion in olive oil until translucent (about 5 minutes), add mustard seeds and tomatoes, and season with salt.

Take the fallen eggplant—skin and all—and the sautéed onion-tomato mix, and put into a food processor. Blend until smooth. Transfer to a bowl and stir in lime juice, garlic, and chopped cilantro. Taste and add more salt as necessary.

Serve with pita chips.

PASTA WITH PUMPKIN
AND FRESH TOMATOES

Makes 6 servings

1 pint cherry tomatoes or
    2 large tomatoes, cut
    in a large dice
Red chili peppers
3 tablespoons olive oil,
    plus more for the pasta
2 garlic cloves, thinly
    sliced
3 tablespoons balsamic
    vinegar
3 tablespoons basil,
    julienned
1 cup cubed pumpkin
1 tablespoon agave or
    honey
1 lemon, juiced
Whole wheat pasta
1 cup arugula
Parmesan cheese, grated

Optional:
8 ounces bacon, sliced
    thin and cooked until
    crispy
2 chicken sausages,
    removed from casings,
    crumbled, and cooked
    until done and browned
    on the outside

This classic recipe never goes out of style. In the summer, when tomatoes are at their peak, I use only tomatoes. In the fall, I add pumpkin. And in the winter, I make it heartier with either bacon or chicken sausages.

In a large bowl, season the tomatoes with salt, pepper, and red chili peppers to taste. Heat olive oil in small skillet, and cook garlic until just browned. Pour hot oil and cooked garlic over the diced tomatoes. Add balsamic vinegar and basil.

Sauté cubed pumpkin in a little oil until soft. Add agave, lemon juice, and salt, and then combine this mixture with the tomatoes.

Meanwhile, cook the whole wheat pasta in a large pot of salted water per package instructions. Drain, toss with a small amount of olive oil, and season with salt and pepper.

Toss the seasoned pasta with the tomato mixture, add in the arugula, and dust with Parmesan cheese.

If you like, add bacon or crumbled chicken sausages.

ROASTED MUSTARD

BRUSSELS SPROUTS

Makes 8 servings

3 cups Brussels sprouts,
   halved lengthwise
   through root
¼ cup olive oil
4 tablespoons whole-
   grain mustard
3 tablespoons mayonnaise

Optional garnish:
Chopped herbs

I think there are only two ways of eating Brussels sprouts, which is either raw (p. 66) or roasted. Once they are roasted, there are several ways to finish them up. The classic way is to just sprinkle them with balsamic vinegar. You can also add bacon and dates, or pork belly and maple syrup. I find that mustard goes very well with Brussels sprouts, which I also use in the raw version.

Drizzle the sprouts with olive oil, place them cut side down on a sheet pan, and then bake them in a preheated 400 degree oven for 20 to 30 minutes, until browned and soft.

Meanwhile, whisk together mustard and mayonnaise. When the sprouts are done, toss with the mustard-mayo mix, and season to taste with salt and pepper.

Garnish with any chopped herbs if desired.

GRILLED SALAD
WITH SALSA DRESSING

Serves 4

⅓ cup olive oil
1 cup salsa, store bought
   or homemade (p. 65)
1 head romaine lettuce,
   cut into quarters

Optional:
Crumbled feta cheese
Sliced avocado
Cooked black beans

Do you have leftover salsa but no chips?
Turn it into a dressing. Just add
olive oil.

In a bowl, slowly whisk the olive oil into the salsa. Voilà: dressing!
   On a hot grill, char the romaine lettuce, cut side down, for 1 minute until the lettuce slightly chars but before it starts to wilt.
   Place the lettuce on a platter, and pour salsa dressing over it. If desired, garnish with feta cheese, sliced avocado, and black beans.

BACON LETTUCE
TOMATO SALAD

6 strips of bacon, cut
   thin
4 cups butter lettuce
½ cup faux Caesar
   dressing (p. 54)
1 pint cherry tomatoes,
   cut in half

Optional garnish:
Croutons

There is the BLT sandwich, and then there is the BLT salad. Can't go wrong with either.

Cook the bacon in a medium skillet until rendered, brown, and crispy. Drain on paper towels.

   Toss the lettuce with the Caesar dressing, and place on a platter. Garnish with bacon and tomatoes. If desired, add croutons.

ORZO WITH PEPPERS, TOMATOES, AND OLIVES

Makes 4 servings

For basil butter:
1 stick butter
3 tablespoons fresh basil
    leaves
1 garlic clove, grated
Zest from one lemon
½ teaspoon red hot chili
    flakes

For orzo:
2 cups orzo, cooked
    according to package
    instructions
½ cup cherry tomatoes,
    cut in half
½ cup red bell peppers,
    cut into strips
½ cup black olives,
    pitted
½ cup chopped parsley

For garnish:
Arugula or radicchio

Orzo is a really easy pasta to cook, especially ahead of time. Eat it at room temperature or heat it up, either in the oven or in a microwave.

In a food processor, combine all basil butter ingredients and pulse until blended.

Toss the hot cooked orzo with about half the basil butter, depending how buttery you like it, and season to taste with salt. Add the remaining ingredients, and garnish with arugula or sliced radicchio. Serve hot or room temperature.

Tip: You'll have leftover basil butter, which you can freeze and use again later. It's delicious on toast, all kinds of veggies, and pretty much anything else.

SEARED FAVA OR GARBANZO BEANS

AKA WANNABE EDAMAME

Makes 4 to 6 servings as
    an appetizer

1 pound fava beans
2 tablespoons olive oil
Sea salt

Fava beans grow really well in Malibu,
but who has time to double peel them?
They first need to come out of their pod,
and then the outer coating. Too much work.
Fresh garbanzo beans also grow well, and
they have a hard outer coating that needs
to come off as well before being consumed.
I have a solution for both.

Heat the oil in a skillet, then add the whole beans and sear for a few minutes until their exterior is slightly blackened.

Toss with some sea salt, and they are ready to serve. Eat them like you would edamame, by biting into the pod/shell and removing the bean inside to eat.

CELERY ROOT WITH ARUGULA AND HORSERADISH CREAM

1 celery root, peeled
  and julienned
Juice from one lemon
½ cup horseradish crème
  fraîche (p. 138)
1 bunch of arugula
1 tablespoon black sesame
  seeds or poppy seeds,
  for garnish

Celery root is funny looking—not that commonly used but very versatile. You can use it raw or cooked, in a salad or a soup. Although it is a root vegetable, it is low in starch, so what's not to love?

Toss the sliced celery root with salt and juice from one lemon. Then add the horseradish crème fraiche, toss in the arugula, and garnish with the black sesame seeds.

POTATO BROCCOLI SOUP

Makes 4 to 6 servings

For soup:
1 large yellow onion,
  peeled and chopped
2 tablespoons olive oil
2 russet potatoes, peeled
  and chopped
10 cups chicken broth,
  purchased or homemade
1 head broccoli, chopped

For seriously lime
  dressing:
Juice from 2 limes
1 clove garlic, grated
2 tablespoons olive oil
1 tablespoon cilantro,
  chopped

Without potatoes, I am totally lost—culinarily speaking. Without potatoes, I always feel a little deprived, never fully satisfied. With potato broccoli soup, I am totally in potato bliss.

In a large stock pot, sauté the onion in the olive oil, until translucent, about 3 minutes. Add the potatoes, and sauté for another couple minutes stirring occasionally. Add the broth and simmer until potatoes are cooked through. Add the broccoli and immediately remove the pot from the heat. Add to a blender, and blend until smooth. Season to taste with salt.

Meanwhile, combine all the dressing ingredients in a small bowl. Pour the soup into individual bowls. Drizzle dressing on top. Serve.

FROM THE HIVE

Bees are very popular in Malibu; everyone has them, wants them, or is researching getting them.

I love bees and find them endlessly fascinating. I am by no means an expert. I took exactly one beekeeping class, in which I learned about the queen bee, who is the ruler of the house, and I also learned about the potential for an evil queen takeover. I was told that the beekeeper must keep checking that the original "marked" queen is the one living in the hive. Wow, it sounded like a Disney movie full of drama! I didn't check my hive that often. And sure enough, when I did, my marked queen was gone, and a new, aggressive queen of questionable heritage had taken her place!

Before I could decide what to do about the situation, the queen and all her followers moved out, leaving behind an empty hive full of honey, so it was super easy to harvest. And I can tell you this: You have never had honey until you have had your own straight from the hive. It is amazingly delicious.

The next year, I got one more hive and new bees. And I still have—cross your fingers—my "marked" docile honeybee queen.

One other thing I learned about bees is that often beekeepers feed them a lot of sugar water. Yes, that is right, the bees make honey to eat, but when the beekeeper strips the hive of the honey to sell, the beekeeper feeds

them sugar water instead. And now everyone is wondering why
the bees are in trouble!

An organic beekeeper's primary goal should be to leave
the bees as much honey as they need to survive the winter,
taking no more than 20 percent of the harvest. Bees can
travel as much as four miles per day in search of pollen.
The honey cannot be marked organic unless the bees are
located within a range where everything they have access to
is grown organically.

Healthy bees eat honey, so please get your honey from a
reliable source. Bruce Lampcov (p. 102/107) from Malibu Honey
sells at the restaurant.

Honey is great in and on so many things. Mixed with butter,
it makes a delicious honey butter; drizzled on cheese, it
turns a platter from so-so to so, so amazing! It also makes
an instant dressing or marinade:

Honey + lemon
Honey + soy sauce
Honey + mustard
Honey + hot sauce
= HONEY JOY

MALIBU HONEY
MARINADE

Makes 2½ cups marinade

For basic marinade:
1 cup locally sourced
  honey
⅔ cup organic soy sauce
  or Bragg Liquid Aminos
1 clove garlic, grated
1-inch piece of fresh
  ginger, grated

Optional:
⅓ cup seasoned rice
  vinegar
1 teaspoon red chili
  flakes
½ cup cilantro
¼ cup organic canola oil

You can use this marinade with chicken, beef, or fish. If I am marinating chicken or fish, I leave it in the soy sauce marinade for only about 1 hour. For a cut such as short ribs, I marinate it in the morning and serve it for dinner.

Blend all ingredients in a blender. I use the basic marinade mostly on chicken. If I prepare beef or fish, I usually add the rice vinegar and often the remaining optional ingredients as well.

Season your chicken, beef, or fish lightly with salt. Although the marinade contains soy sauce, which is salty, the amount of honey in the marinade means that your protein still needs a light coating of salt.

If you are preparing chicken or fish, cook within 1 hour of marinating. Beef can marinate for up to 8 hours.

There is good news and bad news about cooking with honey. The good news is that it gives the meat or fish a gorgeous brown color; the bad news is that it can easily burn. If you are cooking a thin cut of meat or fish, you can cook from start to finish on the grill. If you are cooking a thicker cut or a whole chicken leg, you can sear it until golden brown on the grill, then finish in a pre-heated 375 degree oven until cooked through.

HONEY LEMON SAFFRON

CHICKEN

Makes 4 servings

2 tablespoons butter

1 clove garlic, grated

1 pinch saffron

2 tablespoons honey

1 lemon, juiced

6 chicken thighs,
  boneless and with
  skin on

Saffron has a slightly bitter flavor, which makes it perfect for pairing with honey.

Melt the butter in a small pan, stir in the garlic and saffron, and cook on very low heat for a few minutes. Stir in the honey and lemon juice. Remove from heat and allow to cool.

Season the chicken lightly on both sides with salt, and toss in the marinade. Allow the chicken to marinate overnight.

The next day, either grill the chicken, skin side first, or sauté in a hot skillet, also skin side first, until the skin is super crispy.

If the chicken is not cooked all the way through, finish in a preheated 375 degree oven for 5 minutes.

HONEY BUTTERNUT

SQUASH WITH LIME

Makes 4 servings

1 small butternut squash
    (or pumpkin can be
    substituted)
A little olive oil
Honey to taste
Seriously Lime Dressing,
    optional (page 100)

Butternut squash is a great mashed potato alternative. This recipe contains no butter or cream, so it is a vegan dish. It can be made several days in advance and heated as needed.

Halve the butternut squash. Place cut side down on a sheet pan. Drizzle lightly with olive oil, splash a few tablespoons of water on the sheet pan, and then bake in a preheated 375 degree oven until soft, about 45 minutes.

Peel it and smash it, mash it, or put it into a ricer, if you like. You are making a nice light, fluffy mashed-potato-sort-of-thing.

Season with honey and salt to taste. Depending on the size of your butternut squash, I am going to say to use about 3 tablespoons of honey and ¼ teaspoon of salt.

Eat as is or pour some lime dressing on top.

Tip: Mashed butternut squash goes great in a black bean taco. Heat some corn tortillas in a sauté pan or over an open flame on a gas stove, and then place 2 tablespoons of butternut squash puree on each one. Top with a heaping tablespoon of black beans, followed by salsa and then feta cheese. Fold over and enjoy.

SPICY HONEY
SWEET POTATOES
+ POMEGRANATE

Makes 6 servings

2 large russet potatoes,
  peeled, chopped,
  boiled in salted water
  until soft, drained,
  and then reheated on
  the stovetop for a few
  minutes to cook away
  excess water

1 stick butter

½ cup heavy cream

4 large sweet potatoes,
  baked with the skin on
  until soft

Chili sauce (or sriracha,
  Tabasco, smoky
  habanero sauce, or some
  combination) to taste

½ cup honey

½ cup pomegranate seeds

2 tablespoons chopped
  parsley

My favorite thing about Thanksgiving is not the turkey. No, no, no. I love these spicy sweet potatoes. They're already such a gorgeous color, and when you pour the honey-pomegranate mixture over them, it is time to be thankful. I usually do a 60 percent sweet potato to 40 percent russet potato mix because I like the softer texture better, but you can use all sweet potatoes if you wish.

First, we need to mash the russet potatoes. Push them through a ricer into the bowl of an electric mixer, and then add butter and cream. Season to taste with salt. Now you have a small mound of regular mashed potatoes.

Peel the sweet potatoes and scoop out the soft flesh into the mashed potato mixture. Add hot sauce to taste, and half of the honey.

In a small bowl, combine the rest of the honey with the pomegranate seeds and chopped parsley.

Transfer the potato mixture into a serving bowl. Right before serving, pour the honey-pomegranate mixture over it.

This dish can be made several days ahead and heated in the microwave. Or cover it and place it in a preheated 350 degree oven until heated through, about 10 minutes.

HONEY-BASIL LEMONADE

<u>Makes 2 quarts</u>

1 cup honey
1 cup lemon juice
1 handful lemon basil,
   leaves only
6 cups water

I have several lemon trees, and in the middle of the summer I have a huge harvest. I use lemon every day in my cooking because, as I've said before, there is no such thing as too much lemon. I love my Meyer lemons, but my Eureka lemons are more tart and suitable for lemonade. When life gives you lemons? Add honey—it's super delicious.

In a blender, combine all ingredients, and process until the honey is emulsified in the juice. You can strain out the basil leaves before serving or leave them in—your choice.

KABOCHA SQUASH WITH BLACK LENTILS AND HONEY

Makes 4 servings

1 whole kabocha squash
2 tablespoons olive oil
1 cup black lentils,
   cooked per package
   instructions

For honey lemon dressing:
3 tablespoons honey
¼ cup lemon juice
3 tablespoons olive oil

Optional:
Arugula
Crumbled feta cheese

Cutting into a raw kabocha squash can be challenging, as it is very hard. Boiling it for a few minutes first will soften it significantly and make it easier to manage.

Drizzled with honey lemon dressing and served with black lentils, it makes a great gluten-free side dish. Add arugula and sprinkle with feta cheese for a filling salad.

Place the whole kabocha squash in a large pasta pot, and cover with water. Bring to a boil and simmer for 5 minutes. Drain and cut into wedges, thin or thick. Leave the green skin on or remove it. I prefer to keep it on because it looks prettier.

Drizzle a sheet pan with olive oil, and lay the cut wedges on it. Bake in a preheated 400 degree oven for 20 minutes, turning once halfway through. Season cooked squash wedges with salt.

Whisk together the honey lemon dressing ingredients.

Toss the squash with the dressing and cooked lentils. If desired, garnish with arugula and crumbled feta cheese.

FROM THE DAIRY

I love dairy—not milk so much, but I can't live without cheese or heavy cream. I also love cows and dream that one day I'll have a farm large enough to keep them. I once put a deposit on a miniature zebu cow to bring here to Malibu. I wanted it so badly, but then I realized our property was not large enough for it. One day!

Goats are the next best thing: They are very loyal and really act like dogs, and they are much smaller than cows. And they give the best milk—what's not to love? You can take them on a hike, and the goats will walk right behind you without a leash, following you wherever you go.

Sometimes we take our goats, Casey and Quincy, hiking in the mountains. Sometimes we take them to the beach. They are total beach bums and love to climb the rocks while they watch the surfers.

My friend Danette McReynolds from Chèvre Lavande (p. 129) has a farm, and she makes beautiful soaps and the most delicious cheese.

GOAT CHEESE

Making goat cheese is more about cleaning
and sterilizing than anything else. You
can buy a goat cheese starter, or you can
use lemon juice or distilled vinegar to
curdle the heated goat milk. This is the
same way you also make ricotta cheese,
which you leave in loose curds instead of
packing together into logs.

Never use ultrapasteurized milk for making
cheese; it is too hard to get to curdle.
Most organic milk, unfortunately, is
ultrapasteurized; so raw and straight from
the goat is the easiest way to do it, but
pasteurized will work too.

In this recipe, the acid in the lemon juice
curdles the heated goat milk. But don't
use Meyer lemons for this, as they are not
acidic enough. If you don't have lemons,
you can use vinegar instead.
   Once the liquid is drained away from the
curds, you have a basic but tasty version
of goat cheese.
   Danette often flavors her cheese with
herbs, such as lavender, and seasoned oils.

Makes 4 servings

1 quart goat milk
$\frac{1}{3}$ cup fresh lemon juice
  or distilled vinegar

Optional add-ins:
Herbs, such as rosemary,
  thyme, lavender, or
  sage
Flavorful oils, such as
  walnut oil or sesame
  seed oil

Slowly heat the milk on the stove over medium-high heat until it reaches 180–185 degrees. Gentle bubbles should be forming, and the surface will look foamy. Turn off the heat. You are more likely to underheat the milk than to overheat it. I find that if it will not curdle, it is because the milk is too cold.

Stir in the lemon juice or vinegar, and then let the milk sit for 10 minutes. It should curdle and become slightly thicker on the surface.

Line a colander over a bowl with two layers of cheesecloth. Gently pour the milk into the cheesecloth. Then gather up the cheesecloth around the curds, and tie the curds into a bundle.

Hang the bundle over a pot or jar, so the liquid can drip out. Let the cheese drain for at least 1½ hours.

Scrape the cheese into a bowl. Stir in salt and any optional ingredients to taste.

Use your hands to pat and shape the cheese into a small wheel. The flavor and texture usually improves a bit if you refrigerate it for a few hours before serving.

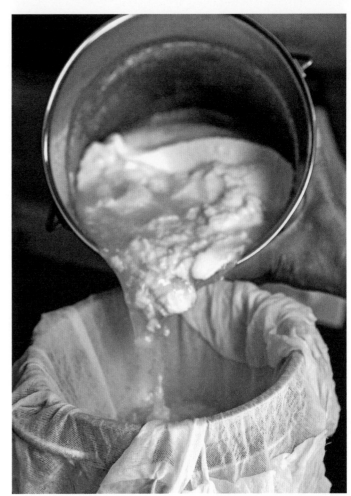

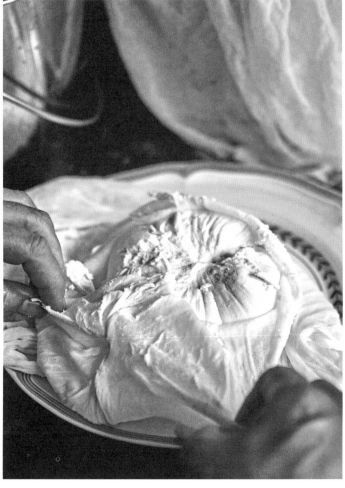

GOAT CHEESE POTATO PIZZA TARTLET WITH MUSHROOMS AND ARUGULA

1 sheet puff pastry—OK,
  you can make yours, but
  I am going to buy mine

½ cup goat cheese

½ cup crème fraîche

1 egg

3 cups three-cheese
  blend, sliced or
  shredded

1 large russet potato,
  sliced thin on a
  mandoline and then
  cooked in salted water
  for 1 to 2 minutes

A drizzle of olive oil

2 tablespoons grated
  Parmesan cheese

1 tablespoon fresh
  rosemary

Handful of mushrooms,
  cooked on high heat
  for a few minutes and
  seasoned with salt and
  pepper to taste

Small bunch of arugula,
  tossed with salt, olive
  oil, and lemon juice to
  taste

Double starch is double delight—baby potatoes in your pasta, because really, what is better than baby potatoes in your pasta? Hmm. Potatoes on your pizza?

Defrost your puff pastry and spread on a sheet pan. It is always a good idea to use a Silpat nonstick baking sheet or parchment paper underneath the puff pastry. Poke the puff pastry with a fork all over to prevent the dough from rising and not cooking through properly.

In a food processor, mix the goat cheese with the crème fraîche and the egg. You want the cheese to become spreadable. Then spread the mixture over the puff pastry, and cover with the sliced or shredded cheese.

Place your potato slices decoratively over the top, drizzle with olive oil, dust with Parmesan cheese, and then sprinkle with rosemary and salt.

Bake the pizza in a preheated 425 degree oven until almost done. Lift the pizza a little, and look at the bottom. It should be nice and brown. It is going to take around 45 minutes, but you are going to have to check it!

When the pizza is almost done, add the mushrooms and return to the oven for a few more minutes. Once it's done (that's right—once it's done), take it out and garnish with the seasoned arugula.

BURRATA, NECTARINE, AND ARUGULA SALAD WITH SESAME SEED CANDY

For sweet pomegranate
  dressing
⅛ cup balsamic vinegar
3 tablespoons
  pomegranate molasses
  or maple syrup
1 teaspoon chopped
  shallot
¼ cup olive oil
Salt to taste

For salad:
1 bunch arugula
4 ripe nectarines or
  peaches, sliced
1 8-ounce ball of burrata
  cheese, shredded

Garnish:
Sesame seed candy (recipe
  follows)
Fresh mint, chopped
Pomegranate seeds

This is a great salad. In the summer, I make it with nectarines or peaches; in the fall, I make it with figs or persimmons. In the winter, I use black grapes. It should be enjoyed all year round.

To make the dressing, whisk together all of the ingredients in a large bowl.

Toss the arugula and the nectarines in the sweet pomegranate dressing, then scatter shreds of burrata cheese on top. (Pouring the dressing over the burrata would give the burrata an unappetizing color, and we don't want that.)

Garnish with sesame seed candy and mint. When they're in season, pomegranate seeds are a great addition, too.

Sesame seed candy:

⅓ cup sugar

½ cup toasted sesame
  seeds

To make sesame seed candy, you just need more seeds than sugar. In a small, dry skillet over medium heat, add ⅓ cup sugar. No need to stir or do anything. Just sit back and wait for it to melt. If it is starting to burn, turn down the heat. Just when the sugar begins to melt, stir in ½ cup toasted sesame seeds.

Once the sugar is fully melted and the sesame seeds are incorporated into it, pour the mixture onto a lightly greased sheet pan and set aside to cool.

Once cool, break or cut into little candy pieces. If you have a hard-as-rock mass of sugar and seeds, you used too much sugar. Toss it out and start again.

CREAMY POTATO AND GREEN TOMATO GRATIN

Makes 4 servings

½ cup heavy cream
1 garlic clove, grated
1 tablespoon chopped
rosemary
2 tablespoons grated
Parmesan cheese
2 large russet potatoes,
sliced thin
2 large tomatoes, sliced
thin

Potato gratin can be a little heavy, so making it half tomato really lightens it up. It is a great use for early green tomatoes, but red will work just fine too. This gratin can be prepared in advance. When you're ready, just pop it in the oven to finish.

In a bowl, mix together heavy cream, garlic, rosemary, and Parmesan cheese. Toss in the sliced potatoes and season lightly with salt (about ¼ teaspoon).

Place in the bottom of a decorative microwave-safe, ovenproof gratin dish. Arrange the tomatoes on top of the potatoes and sprinkle lightly with salt.

OK, please don't tell, but we are going to cheat. . . .

Put it into the microwave for 4 minutes. This is really going to speed up the process. Then finish in the oven at 400 degrees for 20 minutes. You can bake the dish without using the microwave first, but you will need to cover it and bake at a lower temperature (350 degrees) to cook the potatoes through without burning them.

TMZ SALAD

AKA TOMATO, MOZZARELLA,

AND ZUCCHINI SALAD

2 large zucchini,
   sliced very thin on a
   mandoline
Olive oil to taste
1 garlic clove, grated
1 lemon, juiced
1 large mozzarella ball
   or many small ones
3 large ripe tomatoes—or
   cherry tomatoes will
   work too
Drizzle of balsamic
   vinegar
Handful of arugula or
   basil

During summer, the tomato mozzarella salad is everywhere. At the same time, there is zucchini galore in the garden, and so one day I made my caprese into a TMZ—which is a very practical way to update the classic. This salad is all about very simple ingredients, just really good ones. It is imperative that you use excellent mozzarella, ripe tomatoes, and good salt.

Toss the zucchini with salt to taste, olive oil to taste, grated garlic, and lemon juice. Allow to marinate for 10 minutes. Cut the mozzarella ball into medium-thick slices, and then cut the tomatoes into similar-sized slices. If you are using little mozzarella balls or cherry tomatoes, you can leave them whole.

Layer the mozzarella and the sliced tomato on a platter. Sprinkle with salt. Add a splash of olive oil and a drizzle of balsamic vinegar. Then top with the raw zucchini mixture, and garnish with arugula or basil.

HORSERADISH
CRÈME FRAÎCHE

Makes ¾ cup

2 tablespoons
   horseradish
½ cup crème fraîche
Squeeze of lemon
Pinch of salt

Crème fraîche + horseradish = super delish.

This sauce goes great with so many things, including marinated beets (featured here with black sesame seeds and chopped dill), grilled steak, potatoes, and smoked salmon.

Start by adding a little prepared horseradish to the crème fraîche. Keep adding more, tasting as you go along, until the sauce is just the way you like it. (The measurement of 2 tablespoons of horseradish is just a suggestion—it makes for a fairly hot sauce. You might like it milder or even hotter.) Add lemon juice and salt. Stir.

GOAT CHEESE
WITH FRESH FIGS

Makes 4 to 6 servings

For salad:
8-ounce log of goat
    cheese
¼ cup honey or agave
8 ripe figs, halved
Wasa brand Swedish-style
    cracker bread or your
    own favorite cracker or
    toast

For garnish:
Toasted seeds
Sesame seed candy (p. 133)
Toasted nuts

What is better than a cheese platter with fresh fruit and a glass of wine?

You can warm any cheese ever so slightly, giving it that bit of melty warm goodness that really makes a difference.

Warm the goat cheese in a preheated 375 degree oven for 5 minutes. Drizzle with honey or agave. Serve with fresh figs and crackers or toast. Garnish with toasted seeds, sesame seed candy, or toasted nuts.

Tip: This recipe tastes great with brie, too.

LAVASH PIZZA
WITH CAULIFLOWER

Makes 2 regular-size
    servings or 6 appetizer
    servings

½ cup goat cheese or
    ricotta cheese
½ cup crème fraîche
1 egg
A little olive oil
1 piece lavash bread
Shredded three-cheese
    blend
Lots of finely sliced
    cauliflower

This isn't really a pizza at all. It is more of a cracker. A cracker full of bubbling hot cheese and thinly sliced cauliflower.

In a food processor, combine the cheese, crème fraîche, and egg. The exact quantities are not important; you just want to end up with a spreadable cheese mixture.

Brush olive oil on a sheet pan, and lay the lavash bread on top.

Spread goat cheese mixture on lavash bread, distribute shredded cheese over it, and top with lots of finely sliced cauliflower.

Drizzle olive oil on top, and season lightly with salt. Bake in a preheated 450 degree oven until lavash is starting to brown around the edges and get crispy. I am not gonna tell you how long that will take, because it really depends on your oven. Bake it until it is done. Remove from the oven and cut into squares.

TWICE-BAKED
YOGURT POTATOES

4 medium baking potatoes
½ stick butter
½ cup yogurt, crème
   fraîche, or sour cream
1 cup grated Cheddar
   cheese
Chopped herbs, pesto, or
   sun-dried tomato paste
   (optional)

Why do something once when you can do it twice for a better result? These potatoes can be prepared a day in advance and then baked until crispy right before serving.

Score your potatoes down the center and all the way around. This will make it much easier to cut them neatly after they are baked. Then bake your potatoes in a preheated 400 degree oven until they are soft when pierced. How long? It's going to take at least 30 minutes, and maybe as long as 1 hour, so pierce them every now and then to check whether they are soft yet.

Split your baked potatoes in half. Using the score mark will make it easy. Keep them neat, because we are going to stuff them back together. Scoop out most of the flesh and reserve the potato shells. Place the flesh in a large bowl.

Add butter and stir until melted. Season with salt and pepper to taste. Stir in the yogurt and grated Cheddar cheese. If desired, you can add chopped herbs or a squeeze of pesto or sun-dried tomato paste.

Spoon the potato mixture into the reserved empty potato shells. The stuffed potatoes can be made ahead and chilled at this point.

When ready to serve, bake in a preheated 450 degree oven for 10 to 12 minutes, until nice and crispy on top.

FROM THE PASTURE

Grass-Fed Beef

As I already mentioned, I've always wanted a cow; I love their gentle, grazing nature. Left to their own devices, cows are vegan, converting grass into milk and meat, while they produce the absolute best manure for our gardens. The only thing polluting about cows is the way we raise them. Factory farms produce staggering amounts of manure, which can make its way into groundwater.

I don't eat red meat, but every now and then, here on the farm we grill our guests a steak. I always recommend using a premium product—organic and grass-fed beef—and eating smaller portions, less often.

BALSAMIC SKIRT STEAK + CHILI CHERRY TOMATOES

For beef marinade:

½ cup balsamic vinegar

¼ cup olive oil

2 garlic cloves, grated

1 tablespoon fresh herbs, such as a combination of rosemary, basil, and sage

For steak:

3 pounds skirt steak or hanger steak

1 basket cherry tomatoes, halved

1 red chili pepper, thinly sliced

1 tablespoon balsamic vinegar

1 garlic clove, grated

2 tablespoons olive oil

1 bunch arugula or basil

Skirt steak is great party meat because it cooks quickly and can be made to order, but you can use this marinade for any cut of meat.

Combine all marinade ingredients in a blender or whisk together in a bowl. Season the steak lightly with salt on both sides, and pour the marinade over it. Marinate overnight.

Make the garnish by tossing the cherry tomatoes lightly with salt and chili pepper. Stir in the vinegar, garlic, and olive oil.

Grill the steak over high heat for a few minutes per side, then let it rest.

Toss the arugula into the tomato mixture and place on a platter.

Cut the grilled skirt steak into small pieces, and scatter over the arugula-tomato salad.

THE 'BU BETTER BEEF BURGER

Pepperoncini aioli:

1 cup mayonnaise
  (homemade or
  purchased)
¾ cup pepperoncini
  (in a jar)
1 teaspoon chopped
  shallot
3 tablespoons chopped
  flat-leaf parsley
Sprinkle of salt

I don't make beef burgers that often, but sometimes my house gets invaded by my son Casper's skater buddies, and a dozen starving boys are looking for something to eat. Then it is time to whip out the burger. I keep it simple with an 80/20 blend of chuck and brisket, ground very fresh and pretty coarse. Then I just give it some salt, a few turns of the pepper mill, and grill it up.

When we first opened the café, we did not have a beef burger on the menu, but after many requests, we added it. It is one of our best-selling items. We serve it with pepperoncini aioli, Havarti cheese, red onions, tomato, and arugula.

Make your own burger or buy one and dress it up.

We also make a vegetarian portobello mushroom burger using the same toppings and aioli. Just grill the mushrooms, season with salt and lemon juice to taste, and assemble.

To make pepperoncini aioli, blend together all ingredients in a blender or food processor.

GRILLED BUTTERFLY BEEF TENDERLOIN WITH HORSERADISH

Makes 8 to 10 servings

1 whole side of beef
   tenderloin, cut down
   the center but not all
   the way through—just
   deep enough that you
   can open it up and make
   it flat
2 garlic cloves, grated
3 tablespoons olive oil
3 tablespoons fresh
   herbs, chopped
Dried chili flakes to
   taste
Horseradish crème
   fraîche (page 138)

Beef tenderloin is a classic for catered events. Like the little black dress, it is everywhere. The most common way to cook tenderloin for these events is to have a whole side.

You can't grill a whole tenderloin because it will burn before it is cooked through—but if you butterfly the tenderloin by cutting down the center to open it up flat, this makes grilling possible. So much more elegant.

Combine the garlic, olive oil, herbs, and chili flakes in a bowl. Season the steak generously with salt all over, and rub the oil-and-garlic mixture over it.

Grill the tenderloin over high heat on each side for about 4 minutes, or until it is rare in the center. Let it rest for 5 minutes. Then slice thin and serve with horseradish crème fraîche.

Tip: You can sear the steak one day ahead, then finish in a preheated 450 degree oven until it reaches desired doneness, about 30 minutes.

WHOLE ROASTED LAMB WITH ROSEMARY AND GARLIC

Serves 30 guests as part
of a buffet

For marinade:
3 whole bulbs of garlic
2 cups mustard
2 cups olive oil
1 cup lemon juice
2 cups fresh rosemary
   sprigs
2 tablespoons red chili
   flakes

1 whole lamb, 30 pounds
   or smaller, prepped
   by butcher for spit
   roasting

We often work with Gypset, an event planning company (they refer to themselves as event artisans), and they have a very cool whole lamb roast setup. If you do not have a spit roaster, you can usually rent one from an all-purpose rental company. Alternatively, you can use this recipe for a more manageable leg of lamb or rack of lamb. Just be sure to scale the marinade down based on the size of your lamb—or have a lot of leftover.

In a food processor, combine marinade ingredients until finely chopped and mixed.

Season the lamb generously with salt on all sides, and then rub the marinade all over it. Allow the lamb to come to room temperature before beginning to roast it. If using a spit roaster, set up the lamb on the spit. Roast over indirect heat for 5 to 6 hours. If the lamb is not crispy and brown toward the end of the cooking time, baste it with additional olive oil and rerake the coals to increase the heat.

The lamb is done when it reaches an internal temperature of 155 degrees.

MIKE GARDNER'S
SAUSAGE

Makes about 20 ¼-pound
   sausages

4 pounds wild boar meat or
   domestic pork
1 pound pork shoulder with
   nice amounts of fat
2 tablespoons sugar
2 tablespoons kosher salt
1 tablespoon garlic powder
1 tablespoon dried thyme
1 tablespoon minced fresh
   sage
1½ tablespoons fennel
   seeds
1 tablespoon red pepper
   flakes
½ cup ice water
About 20 sausage casings
   (ask your local butcher)

This recipe is best when using a young wild boar (under 150 pounds) that smells clean when butchering. One way to test the flavor is to cook a small piece of meat and see if it smells like "good pork." You will need a sausage grinder to make this recipe.

The key to good sausage is keeping everything cold. Start by putting the meat in the freezer for about 1 hour to firm it up. Then cut it into 1-inch cubes.

Combine the sugar, salt, garlic powder, herbs, fennel seeds, and chili flakes, then mix it into the meat.

Grind the meat using a coarse die and let it fall into a bowl that is sitting on top of a large bowl of ice. Add the ice water and mix with your hands for a few minutes, then place it in the fridge while you prepare the casings and put the stuffing attachments on your grinder.

Run the meat through the grinder, stuffing the casing all at once. (If you have never seen or done this, do a Youtube search to see an example.) Twist the links every 7 inches in one direction, and then with the next link, the other direction. Hang the sausages in a cool place (under 58 degrees) for a few hours to tighten them up. Use butcher string to tie off groups of four if vacuum packing for a deep freezer.

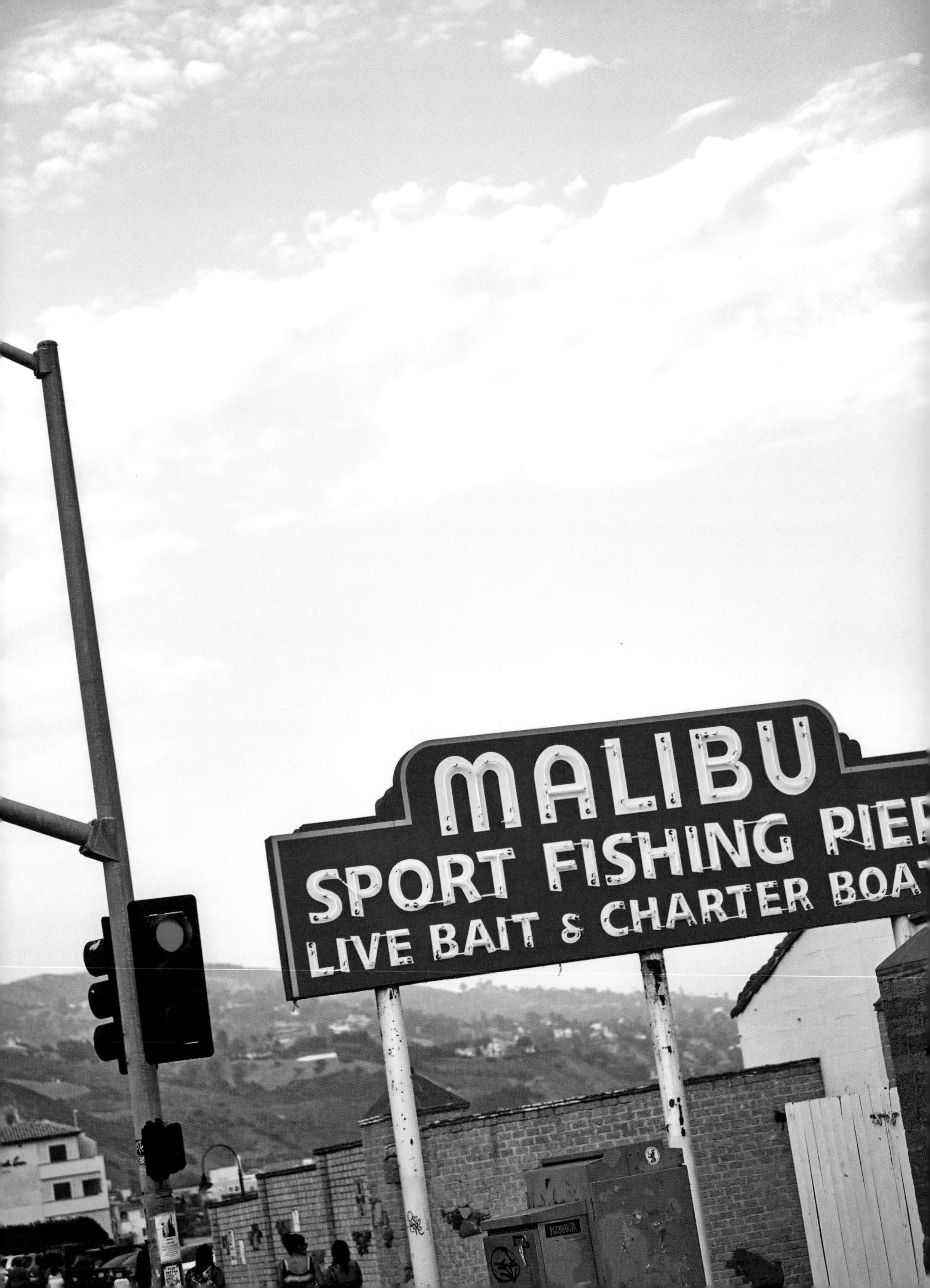
MALIBU
SPORT FISHING PIER
LIVE BAIT & CHARTER BOAT

FROM THE SEA

and on the beach

Obviously, Malibu is all about the ocean and the beaches.

You can fish off the Malibu pier, and many do. Our café is located at the end of the pier, and so the fishermen are a daily presence in our life here. Sometimes they catch big rays or sharks, which upsets some of our customers who are not accustomed to seeing large sea creatures captured right in front of them. Fishing is, however, legal on the Malibu pier—in fact, it is officially called the Malibu Sport Fishing Pier.

Some ultracool locals, including my friend Mike Gardner (above and p. 158), swim out with a spear gun in designated areas and catch excellent sea bass off the coast. There are also a lot of lobsters off the coast of Malibu, and you can often find the beaches scattered with their shells. Crazily enough, all the Malibu lobsters are shipped to China and Japan, and the lobsters for sale in Malibu are from the East Coast—go figure.

Malibu has a great little fish market, Malibu Seafood, right on the Pacific Coast Highway, and it is very popular and always packed.

A visit to the beach in Malibu requires a towel, a surfboard, and a beach picnic—because when the weather is beautiful, you are there to stay and need nutrition to last you all day.

BRANZINO
WITH SALSA VERDE

Makes 4 servings

4 skin-on branzino
  fillets
½ cup capers
2 garlic cloves, grated
3 tablespoons oregano or
  marjoram
3 tablespoons parsley
3 tablespoons olive oil

Branzino, also know as European sea bass or loup de mer, is a small white fish that's easy to cook. At the café we serve it with broccoli mashed potatoes (p. 71) and an arugula garnish—I like to keep the dish all green.

With a sharp knife, score the skin of the branzino in three evenly spaced places. This will help the skin crisp, and prevent the fish from curling up.

Season lightly with salt. Heat a skillet and add the fish fillets, skin side down, without crowding the pan. You may only be able to do two fillets at a time, depending on the size of your pan. Cook until brown and crispy, about 3 minutes. Then turn and cook for about one additional minute or until the fish is cooked through.

Meanwhile, to make the salsa verde, chop the remaining ingredients finely and combine. Alternatively you can use a food processor.

Serve the branzino fillets topped with the salsa.

WHITE SEA BASS IN SOY SAUCE MARINADE WITH GINGER

Makes 6 to 8 servings

3 pounds white sea bass
Sushi ginger
Fresh herbs (parsley,
   chervil, dill)

For soy sauce marinade:
⅓ cup honey
¼ cup organic soy sauce
   or Bragg Liquid Aminos
¼ cup seasoned rice
   vinegar
1 garlic clove, minced
Dried red chili pepper to
   taste
1 two-inch piece of fresh
   ginger
Half a bunch of cilantro,
   chopped

This is a great recipe you can use on locally caught white sea bass or really any fleshy fish.

Don't overmarinate the fish (no longer than 1 hour), or it might turn into ceviche!

Make the marinade by combining all ingredients in a blender or food processor until blended.

Season the sea bass lightly with salt on both sides. Pour most of the marinade over the fish, but reserve a few tablespoons to drizzle over the cooked fish. Marinate for up to 1 hour.

Grill the fish over high heat for 3 minutes per side or until it has a nice brown char to it, and then finish by baking it in a preheated 375 degree oven for 5 more minutes or until done.

Drizzle remaining marinade over the fish, and garnish with sushi ginger and fresh herbs.

Tip: You can prepare the fish one day in advance. Grill it briefly to sear it, but leave it mostly raw, and then place it in the fridge to cool. When you are ready to serve it, take the preseared fish out of the fridge, and bake for 10 minutes or until cooked through. Great for parties—all the messy work has been done beforehand.

MISO-MARINATED

BLACK COD

Makes 6 to 8 servings

For marinade:
⅛ cup mirin
⅛ cup sake
½ cup miso
⅓ cup sugar

3 pounds black cod
Olive oil spray
Sushi ginger
Sesame seeds
Chopped herbs (chives,
   parsley, or cilantro)

Miso is an excellent fish marinade—I think almost everyone likes it. Pairing it with cod is a classic, though it tastes great on salmon, too. The flavor is pretty mellow, so it is best to allow the fish plenty of time to marinate, ideally overnight.

Because the marinade does contain sugar, be careful not to burn the fish as you cook it. Lightly charring it first and then finishing it in the oven works best. You can also broil it.

Combine mirin, sake, miso, and sugar in a small pan, and heat until sugar is dissolved. Allow to cool.

Place fish and marinade in a container for a minimum of 6 hours or preferably overnight.

Grill fish over high heat; spray grill with olive oil spray to prevent sticking. Then transfer to a preheated 375 degree oven to finish.

Garnish with sushi ginger, sesame seeds, and chopped herbs.

SHRIMP WITH FARRO AND WHITE BEANS

1 cup farro, cooked in
   broth or salted water,
   until just right (about
   15 minutes)
1 cup large white beans,
   the bigger the better
½ cup olive oil
2 lemons, juiced
1 garlic clove, grated
Lots of fresh herbs, such
   as parsley, dill, or
   cilantro
1 small Persian cucumber,
   chopped fine
2 stalks celery, chopped
   fine
1 small shallot, chopped
   fine
2 cups arugula
½ cup chopped cherry
   tomatoes
1 pound peeled raw shrimp
2 teaspoons salt
A little olive oil
3 tablespoons dill
   butter: 3 tablespoons
   butter, combined with
   chopped dill and garlic

There are so many cool grains out there that there's no reason to get stuck on the potato, pasta, rice merry-go-round. Step off the carousel. Farro is grain-tastic and one of the healthier kinds out there—chewy and a little crunchy.

Toss the cooked farro and beans together in a bowl, and stir in the olive oil, lemon juice, garlic, and herbs.

Season with salt to taste, and add the cucumber, celery, shallot, arugula, and tomatoes.

Season the shrimp with salt, toss with a little olive oil, and grill or sauté over high heat until just done.

Immediately put the hot shrimp in a bowl with the dill butter, and toss until the butter melts.

Then toss the shrimp in with the farro mixture. Dill-icious!

HALIBUT SANDWICHES WITH BLACK OLIVE AIOLI

You can make a fish sandwich with any type of fish you have—salmon, sea bass, halibut, tuna, and so on. I like to keep mine super simple and then smother it in some super yummy black olive aioli.

Every year there is a golf cart Fourth of July parade in my Malibu neighborhood. The parade is hilarious in this very small town. Every single person who lives here is in the parade, so there are no spectators, which I find amusing.

The first year, we decorated our golf cart using a farm theme and went home with no prize. The second year, we went with a surf theme and had the same result—no ribbon. Then it dawned on me that I was making up my own themes when the theme was the Fourth of July. The third year, we went all out with red, white, and blue—100 percent kitsch, no style, no substance. Just a pure, over-the-top blast—and we emerged with the grand prize! We celebrated our Fourth of July golf cart parade victory with grilled fish sandwiches.

Makes 4 sandwiches

4 6-ounce cut halibut
   fillets (although any
   fish can be used)
4 brioche burger buns
Baby arugula
Tomatoes, sliced
Red onion, chopped
Black olive aioli
   (p. 210)

Season fish lightly with salt, and pan sear or grill. Toast the brioche burger buns, and put some arugula on the bottom. Add tomato or onion. Place the cooked fish on top, and smear it with a large dollop of black olive aioli. Top with the bun and celebrate!

PARSNIP-POTATO LATKES

Makes 8 servings

2 large russet potatoes,
  peeled
2 large parsnips, peeled
½ lemon, juiced
A little flour, about
  2 tablespoons
Olive oil
½ cup horseradish crème
  fraîche (p. 138)
½ pound smoked salmon

I love potatoes in every variation, and crispy latkes are definitely a favorite. I also love parsnips—an underutilized root vegetable with a sweet, slightly earthy and nutty taste. The combination is the best of both worlds, and the perfect backdrop for smoked salmon.

Coarsely grind potatoes and parsnips in a food processor, or shred them using a grater. Place on a kitchen towel, and wring out any juices. Sprinkle with lemon juice to prevent browning.

Toss with a little flour to help the potatoes and parsnips stick together and form into mini pancakes with your hands.

Fry the latkes in a preheated skillet with a little olive oil until browned, about 1 minute. Flip and repeat on the opposite side.

Latkes can be made in advance and frozen, which is what I always do for our holiday breakfast. They can go straight from the freezer to a preheated 375 degree oven for 10 minutes or until crispy and hot.

Serve with horseradish crème fraîche and smoked salmon.

Tip: If you like, partially cook the potatoes and the parsnips, then chill them before grating them and proceeding as above. This trick gives the latkes a slightly softer texture.

GRILLED LOBSTER
+ LIME BUTTER

You want oohs and ahhs? Bring out a big platter of grilled lobsters; your guests will be super impressed.

We did grilled lobsters for 200 guests for a Valentine's Day dinner. Easy. We got the fishmonger to split them for us, and they delivered them in time to go straight on the grill.

The most humane way—for both the human and the lobsters—to do the deed that must be done is to place the live lobsters in the freezer until they go to sleep, but before they are totally frozen, about 1 hour. Then quickly split the lobsters in half. You can keep the split lobsters in the fridge for a few hours, but they should be cooked and eaten as soon as possible.

recipe continues

4 live lobsters, chilled
  and then split in half
  lengthwise
4 sticks of butter
Additional 2 sticks of
  butter, softened
1 bunch cilantro
Jalapeño pepper to taste
Juice and zest from
  1 lime

OK, I know, it sounds like a lot of butter. Relax; we are going to make a butter bath *and* a seasoned butter.

The only tricky thing about grilling lobsters is that the tail meat cooks much quicker than the claws. Just follow along—it's super easy.

Bring a pot of salted water to boil. When boiling, dip the claws into the boiling water, keeping the rest of the body out of the water, until they turn pink. Remove.

Chop the 4 sticks of butter into little pieces. Then bring 4 tablespoons of water to a boil in a skillet, and whisk in one little piece of butter at a time. It should emulsify to a thick, frothy butter bath. Keep adding all the butter. Once it's all melted, keep the skillet on very low heat, and place the lobsters, flesh down, into the butter for a few minutes until barely cooked through. Remove from the butter bath, and place on a sheet pan. Season the flesh lightly with salt.

To make the lime butter, combine the 2 sticks of softened butter with cilantro, jalapeño pepper, and lime juice and zest in a food processor, or blend by hand using a fork until all ingredients are combined. Set aside.

Preheat the grill and once it is hot, place each lobster, flesh down, on it for 1 minute until charred, and then flip to cook the shell side. Place a generous scoop of lime butter into the shell, and cook until melted. Serve at once.

Tip: Make the lime butter ahead of time and freeze it.

ALASKA-CAUGHT TRUE COD WITH ROCK SHRIMP BEURRE BLANC

4 medium-size true cod
  fillets, lightly salted
1 tablespoon butter
2 tablespoons olive oil

For rock shrimp beurre
  blanc:
½ pound raw rock shrimp
1 teaspoon chopped
  shallot
½ cup dry white wine or
  sake
¼ cup pickled sushi
  ginger
1 cup heavy cream
4 tablespoons butter
3 tablespoons chopped
  fresh dill

True cod caught in Alaska waters are a Monterey Bay Aquarium Seafood Watch "best choice," as they are hook-and-line caught and are sustainable. Most recipes call for turning true cod into fish and chips—but why? Even our seafood supplier asked if we had bought a fryer when we ordered true cod for the café. True cod is totally delicious when lightly sautéed. This way of cooking the fish showcases its light, mild, sweet flavor and flaky texture.

Sauté the true cod fillets in butter and olive oil in a large skillet. Cook for 2 minutes per side until lightly browned and cooked through. Don't crowd your skillet. Cook only 2 fillets at a time, if necessary. Remove cod from skillet.

Cook the rock shrimp in the same pan for about 4 minutes.

To make the beurre blanc, add shallot and wine to a small pan. Cook until the wine reduces to just a few tablespoons. Add the pickled ginger and heavy cream. Cook for about 5 minutes until reduced. Remove from heat and whisk in the butter until incorporated. Season lightly with salt, and stir in chopped dill and cooked shrimp.

Pour the sauce over the cooked fish fillets and rock shrimp and serve.

SALMON + GRAINY
MUSTARD DRESSING

Makes 8 to 10 servings

1 whole side of salmon
Sushi ginger
Herbs or arugula

For grainy mustard
  dressing:
2 tablespoons whole-
  grain mustard
2 tablespoons Bragg
  Liquid Aminos or soy
  sauce
1 garlic clove, grated
4 tablespoons olive oil

I love mustard—you can mix it with so many things to make the best marinades and dressings. Mustard with honey and mustard with soy sauce are basic sauces you can never go wrong with.

I especially love whole-grain mustard mixed with honey, soy sauce, or both.

Grill or sauté the salmon until it is just done. Leave it a little pink in the center. No need to season it with salt—both mustard and soy sauce are salty.

While the salmon is cooking, whisk together the dressing ingredients in a bowl.

Pour the dressing over the salmon, and garnish with the sushi ginger and the herbs or arugula.

SHRIMP WITH CARROT-GINGER COCONUT SAUCE

Makes 4 to 6 servings

For coconut sauce:
1 (14-ounce) can
   coconut milk
1 medium carrot, chopped
1 half-a-thumb-sized
   piece of ginger
1 garlic clove
1 serrano pepper or to
   taste
3 tablespoons organic soy
   sauce or Bragg Liquid
   Aminos
1 cup fresh cilantro or
   parsley
2 limes, juiced
1 small piece fresh
   turmeric (optional)
1 stalk lemongrass
   (optional)

2 tablespoons olive oil
1 pound rock shrimp
Any mix of vegetables:
   bell pepper, organic
   corn, onion, snap peas,
   asparagus, and so on

This coconut sauce also goes well with vegetables and tofu, and we use it all the time as a vegan alternative at our events. It can be made several days in advance and then heated and poured over your ingredients of choice just before serving. This dish is best served with rice, quinoa, or some other grain that can absorb the sauce.

To the blender or food processor, add all of the ingredients for the sauce. Include turmeric and lemongrass if you like. Whirl, blend, yum yum. Taste for seasoning and maybe add a dash of salt or a tiny bit more soy sauce. Maybe.

In batches, and in a little olive oil over high heat, sauté the shrimp and veggies together until just done. Season with salt and pepper.

Gently heat the coconut sauce. Do not bring to a full boil, as it may break. When hot, pour over the shrimp and vegetables.

Tip: Try this dish with cubed chicken or tofu.

MUSTARD CRAB CAKES

Makes 4 regular-size
   crab cakes
   or 8 appetizers

For crab cakes:
½ pound crabmeat
1 tablespoon mayonnaise
2 teaspoons Dijon mustard
Splash of Tabasco
½ egg (you can put a full
   egg in, but then you
   are going to need more
   bread crumbs)
1 tablespoon bread crumbs
   or just enough to make
   the crab cake hold
   together
Organic cornflake crumbs,
   panko, or bread crumbs
1 tablespoon butter
1 tablespoon olive oil

For caper aioli:
¼ cup mayonnaise
1 teaspoon mustard
1 tablespoon chopped
   capers
1 teaspoon chopped
   shallot
1 teaspoon chopped dill
Pinch of salt

I don't make crab cakes that often, but when I do, I am all about the crab—as in mostly crab, almost no bread filler. I would rather eat a small crab cake that is all crab than a large crab cake that is full of bread. You know?

Into the food processor go the crab, mayo, mustard, Tabasco, egg, and bread crumbs. Whirl and blend. Or mix in a bowl.

With your hands, form into whatever size crab cakes you would like. Coat with cornflake crumbs or any crumb of your choice, such as panko or bread crumbs.

Either bake or sauté in butter and olive oil for a few minutes, until crispy and heated through.

Meanwhile, make the caper aioli. Stir together all the ingredients to combine. Top the crabcakes with caper aioli and serve hot.

THE ULTIMATE

BEACH PICNIC

Living in Malibu means living near the ocean and going to the beach. Knowing what to pack in a beach basket is something every resident has to learn. Every visitor you have—and when you live in Malibu, you will have visitors year-round—will want to go to the beach.

You'll find yourself there longer than you intended, as time simply slips away while you are next to the waves. Take a beach picnic with you, or hunger will force you home before you want to go.

Here are some of my best suggestions to
bring with you:

Mama Tran's Vietnamese chicken salad
(p. 240) goes very well as a picnic, as the
salad can be tossed with dressing ahead
of time.

Chicken salad with olives on country
bread is great, too (p. 226).

The Kale Caesar (p. 54) holds up well in
the heat. Seaweed sugar snap peas (p. 201)
are also a terrific snack.

Or try pretzel baguettes with honey, brie,
and prosciutto for a super simple sandwich.

Sliced turkey is fantastic with cranberry
aioli—just mix 1 cup of cooked cranberry
sauce with 1 cup of mayo. Put it all on
whole wheat bread with some arugula.

Turn the TMZ salad (p. 137) into a
sandwich if you like!

SEAWEED

SUGAR SNAP PEAS

Makes 4 servings

1 pound sugar snap peas
  (trim the string, but
  leave the ends)
1 teaspoon salt
¼ cup finely sliced dried
  seaweed

Crispy sugar snap peas are a perfect beach picnic vegetable.

Place the sugar snap peas in a colander, and pour hot water over them, about 8 cups. Doesn't really matter how much water. I like them raw . . . but just taking the raw edge off makes it so much easier to eat a lot of them. Cooking them in hot water would make them *too* cooked—so a quick hot water bath creates the best of both worlds.

Let them dry. Toss with the salt and the seaweed.

Head to the beach and enjoy!

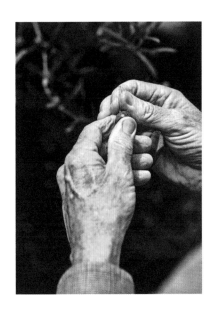

FROM THE OLIVE GROVE

Olive trees dot the Malibu hillsides and backyards across town. Their drought tolerance and the beauty of their silvery foliage and twisted trunks make them a great addition to the landscape. And the oil from the squeezed olives is liquid gold.

My friend Robert Jaye makes the most delicious olive oil—pleasantly bitter with a grassy, fruity aroma and a robust, pungent finish. It's cold pressed from trees that are spread over the city of Malibu, and sold under the label Malibu Olive Company. Robert planted his first olive trees on land next to his family home in Malibu and now has 350 under cultivation.

Recently, I had the most amazing lunch at the Romanelli estate in Malibu, near the local high school. Romanelli is the best-selling label of the Malibu Olive Company brand; the property is dotted with huge olive trees. My meal consisted only of bread, oven-roasted tomatoes, and oil. It was so simple, but one of the most memorable I have had in a long time.

You can replace butter with olive oil in lots of recipes, even desserts. Try it in cakes and pancake batters. The recipes in this chapter highlight and showcase the ingredient or where it comes from.

RAW ZUCCHINI SALAD

For salad:
2 large, very fresh
  zucchini
2 tablespoons good
  olive oil
1 lemon, juiced
1 small garlic clove,
  grated

For garnish:
2 tablespoons fresh
  herbs, such as dill,
  parsley, or chives
Cheese, such as goat
  cheese or feta
Seeds, such as agave-
  sweetened pepitas or
  sunflower seeds
Cooked grains, such as
  quinoa or couscous

I love raw zucchini. So much better than cooked! I can handle only a limited amount of cooked zucchini each summer. But raw—I never get tired of it. Sometimes I slice it super thin on the mandoline; sometimes I use a spiral cutter to make it into long, pretty ribbons.

Slice zucchini as thin as you can, either with a mandoline or a spiral slicer, into the shape of your choice. Toss with a little salt and pepper and with olive oil. Then add lemon juice and garlic.

Eat as is or top with herbs, cheese, seeds, a grain, or some combination of these. The more you add, the heartier the salad becomes.

RICE WITH LENTILS

1 cup jasmine rice
1 cup green or black
    French lentils
2 tablespoons good
    olive oil
Juice and zest of 2 limes
1/2 cup chopped chives
1 tablespoon finely
    chopped red onion
1 tablespoon finely
    chopped dill

Optional:
Thinly sliced raw
    zucchini
Chopped, cooked green
    beans
Lightly steamed
    asparagus, cut into
    2-inch pieces

I am a huge fan of mixing ingredients while keeping it simple. Seasoning your cooked jasmine rice with good olive oil and salt really makes a difference. I stir olive oil into brown rice as well, and toss it with sliced, toasted almonds and parsley.

Cook your rice in salted water or broth per package instructions. At the same time, cook your lentils in salted water or broth, also per package instructions, but try not to overcook either one. Always better to undercook than overcook. If the rice and lentils are too soft and mushy, they will make a mess.

Stir together cooked rice and cooked, drained lentils. Toss well in olive oil, and then season with salt, lime juice and zest, chives, red onions, and dill.

If desired, add zucchini, green beans, and/or asparagus. Serve hot or at room temperature.

BLACK OLIVE AIOLI

Makes 1½ cups

1 cup mayonnaise
¼ cup pitted black
    Kalamata olives
½ cup flat-leaf parsley
1 garlic clove, peeled
1 tablespoon red onion or
    shallot
Pinch of salt

This is such a great and quick dip to make. It goes well with fish or crudités, and can be made several days in advance.

Into the food processor everything goes—but wait, stop! Don't overprocess. Leave it a bit on the chunky side.

ROASTED CAULIFLOWER
WITH OLIVES AND
CHERRY TOMATOES

<u>Makes 4 servings</u>

1 head cauliflower, broken
   into florets and tossed
   with olive oil
1 basket cherry tomatoes
1 cup pitted olives
½ cup lemon dressing
   (p. 215)
1 cup arugula

I love cauliflower. There are really only two ways to cook it, I think: grilled (see the charred cauliflower alternative to charred broccoli, p. 76) or roasted.

Once cauliflower has been roasted, you can keep it super simple with just lemon and arugula, or you can dress it up by adding bacon and dates, or cherry tomatoes and olives, or green beans. So many options—all excellent.

Place the cauliflower on a sheet pan, and roast in a preheated oven at 400 degrees for 30 to 40 minutes, until it starts to brown and becomes soft. Turn it every now and then to brown evenly.

When the cauliflower is almost done, add the whole cherry tomatoes and olives to the sheet pan, and continue to roast until the tomatoes are just starting to burst—about 5 additional minutes.

Season with salt and toss with the lemon dressing.

Finish by adding the arugula and stirring just to wilt.

GREEK QUINOA SALAD

Makes 4 servings

For lemon dressing:
1 small sprig fresh
  oregano leaves
1 garlic clove, grated
2 lemons, juiced
Splash of olive oil
Salt to taste

For salad:
1 basket of cherry
  tomatoes or 2 large
  tomatoes, cut in half
2 small cucumbers, cubed
  (I like to use Persian,
  but any cucumber
  will do)
1 pound Feta cheese,
  cubed
1 bell pepper, any color,
  diced
¼ cup diced red onion
1 cup pitted olives
½ cup chopped parsley
1 cup cooked quinoa

Quinoa is such a great way to add some protein to a basic salad and make it more substantial. A good olive oil and a squeeze of lemon rev up the deliciousness factor.

Whisk together the dressing ingredients in a bowl.

Toss the chopped salad ingredients together in a separate bowl, add the quinoa, and pour the dressing on top. Be sure to taste for seasoning.

The salad is best if it sits out at room temperature for 30 minutes before being served.

215

GREEN BEANS
+ CARROTS

Makes 4 servings

1 bunch carrots, cut in
 half lengthwise
5 tablespoons extra-
 virgin olive oil
2 tablespoons honey or
 agave
1 lemon, juiced
2 cups very thin and
 fresh green beans
1 garlic clove, grated
1 tablespoon balsamic
 vinegar
Herbs, sliced almonds,
 sunflower seeds,
 pepitas, or black
 sesame seeds

Thin green beans with roasted carrots is one of my catering staples. Using a great olive oil really brings out the flavor of the veggies. We are going to work with a 50/50 mix of carrots and green beans. Doesn't really matter how much you are making.

Drizzle your carrots with 3 tablespoons olive oil, and season lightly with salt. Place them cut side down on a sheet pan and roast in a preheated 400 degree oven until lightly browned and barely soft, about 20 minutes. Drizzle with some honey or agave and a squeeze of lemon.

Meanwhile, boil or steam your very thin and gorgeously fresh green beans until just done, about 2 minutes. Leave them crispy. They should be fresh enough to eat raw, so they really need just a quick cook. Drain them, then either plunge them in ice water or rinse in cool water. Toss the green beans with 2 more tablespoons olive oil, and season with garlic and a splash of balsamic.

Toss in the cooked carrots. Garnish with herbs, almonds, sunflower seeds, pepitas, black sesame seeds, or some combination of these.

CRISPY OKRA

¼ cup olive oil
2 cups okra, sliced
  lengthwise

Okra is a love-it-or-hate-it vegetable, thanks to a little thing called slime. But when the okra is cut in half lengthwise and cooked over high heat, the slime disappears and okra skeptics become converts. This is really the simplest of recipes. In fact, it is not even a recipe; it is more of an instruction. Always keep your okra dry, as wetness is what brings out the slime factor.

Heat your olive oil until hot but not smoking in a skillet. Add the okra, cut side down, and cook until nicely browned. Flip over. Done.

The only thing that can go wrong is that you overcook it, and then the slime comes out, so keep the okra crispy and just charred.

Sprinkle with salt and it is ready to eat.

OVEN-DRIED TOMATOES

12 ripe Roma tomatoes,
   cut in half lengthwise
3 tablespoons good olive
   oil

This is another uncomplicated recipe; the only thing that matters is to have the best of ingredients. We had oven-dried tomatoes made with Malibu Olive Company oil, with additional fresh oil to use for dipping in bread, when we joined Robert Jaye for lunch underneath the olive trees at the Romanelli estate. It was a simple but memorable meal.

Coat the tomatoes in olive oil, and sprinkle with salt to taste. Roast in a preheated oven at about 200 degrees for 12 hours.

Serve with bread and with more olive oil for dipping. Now it's like you were there!

GRILLED SMASHED POTATOES + ROASTED GARLIC AND PARMESAN

Makes 4 servings

8 medium to large
  fingerling potatoes,
  which are still way
  smaller than a russet
6 garlic cloves, whole
  and peeled
⅓ cup olive oil or just
  enough to cover the
  garlic
2 tablespoons butter
Fresh, fine-chopped
  rosemary to taste
½ cup grated Parmesan
  cheese

I love baby potatoes simply boiled and sautéed for a minute, but that works best with very small potatoes. Sometimes—especially when you grow your own—oops, they are larger than you wished. This mistake is delicious in a rough smash with olive oil, roasted garlic, and Parmesan cheese.

Boil the potatoes with their skin on in salted water until just soft (about 10 minutes but it depends on size). Then cool and peel. Resist the urge to peel before boiling them. The peel protects the potato from absorbing too much water, and leaving it on will give you a better final product. But do peel them afterward.

Meanwhile, place the garlic in the smallest skillet or pan you have and cover with olive oil. (The smaller the pan you use, the less oil you will need, so the smaller the better.) Cook over very low heat until the garlic is soft and browned. You could roast the garlic, but cooking it on the stovetop is much faster.

In a large bowl, smash the cooked and peeled potatoes with the roasted garlic, the olive oil that the garlic was cooked in, and butter. Season liberally with salt and pepper, add some fresh rosemary, and shower with grated Parmesan.

You can either bake this in a preheated 400 degree oven until browned and crispy, or you can put the container on the grill. You can then call them grilled smashed potatoes—works great in a paella pan.

ROSEMARY WHOLE WHEAT OLIVE OIL CAKE

Makes 8 servings

Makes 8 servings

½ cup whole almonds,
  skin on
1 cup whole wheat flour
¼ teaspoon baking soda
¼ teaspoon baking powder
½ teaspoon kosher salt
1 sprig fresh rosemary
1 cup sugar
½ cup extra-virgin
  olive oil
¼ cup canola oil
¼ cup lemon juice
½ cup plus 2 tablespoons
  milk
2 eggs

For serving:
Whipped cream
Berries

For the baking pan:
Butter, flour

Though I don't have the patience for measuring, sifting, or precision, as a caterer I always had to provide desserts. Many years ago I asked my friend Trevor Zimmerman for a foolproof cake recipe, and he gave me a recipe for olive oil cake. Over the years, I have updated it by using only whole wheat flour and adding more almonds. Sometimes I switch the lemon juice for apple or orange, or the rosemary to bay leaf, or the almonds for walnuts. It's easily adaptable.

In a food processor, finely chop the almonds, then combine with the whole wheat flour. Add the baking soda, baking powder, and salt. Set aside.

Whirl the rosemary with the sugar in the food processor until just combined. In a large bowl, add the rosemary sugar to the oils, lemon juice, milk, and eggs.

Combine wet ingredients with dry ingredients, and place in a buttered and floured 8 X 8 inch baking pan. Bake in a preheated 375 degree oven until a toothpick inserted in the middle of the cake comes back clean (about 45 minutes).

Remove from oven and allow to cool.

Serve with whipped cream and berries. Of course!

Tip: The cake can be made in advance, wrapped in plastic, and frozen.

CHICKEN SALAD SANDWICHES WITH BLACK OLIVE AIOLI

Makes 3 sandwiches

2 cups black olive aioli
   (p. 210)
3 cups cooked, shredded
   chicken
1 cup shredded radicchio
6 slices bread or
   3 mini-baguettes

I love recipes with multiple uses: Make something and use it several different ways. Leftovers turn into brand-new dishes.

The black olive aioli is such a great recipe because you can do so many things with it. Use it as a crudité dip, slather it on a fish sandwich (p. 175), or toss it with shredded cooked chicken for a mouthwatering sandwich.

Combine the black olive aioli with the cooked chicken and the radicchio.

Spread a generous portion between two pieces of bread of your choice. Yum-yum.

GREEN BEANS WITH ROASTED ROMANESCO

Makes 4 servings

1 head romanesco
¼ cup olive oil
2 pounds thin green beans
½ cup lemon juice
Salt to taste

Another great vegetable combination is green beans and romanesco. This veg is reminiscent of cauliflower, but bright green, crunchy, delicate, and nutty.

Break your romanesco into florets. Toss it with half of the olive oil, place on a sheet pan, and roast in a 400 degree preheated oven for 20 minutes or until just beginning to soften and brown. Season with salt to taste.

Meanwhile, in a large pot of salted water, cook your green beans for 2 minutes, then drain and plunge into ice water or rinse under cold water.

Combine the roasted romanesco and the beans. Season with the remaining olive oil, lemon juice, and salt to taste.

ROASTED PORTOBELLOS WITH ROASTED RED PEPPER PESTO

Makes 4 servings

1 garlic clove, roasted
    and chopped
3 tablespoons olive oil
2 tablespoons balsamic
    vinegar
4 large portobello
    mushrooms

Roasted red pepper pesto:
1 red bell pepper
1 Roma tomato
1 tablespoon sriracha or
    other hot sauce
1 teaspoon agave
1 tablespoon balsamic
    vinegar
2 tablespoons olive oil

Vegans and vegetarians are starting to be everywhere, as well as the gluten-free, and the no-carbs. It is hard to always have something that pleases everyone. At the café we make a portobello mushroom "steak" served either with grainy mustard sauce (p. 188) or with roasted red pepper pesto, as here.

The mushrooms can be marinated and baked several days in advance. Reheat for a few minutes in a sauté pan or the microwave.

Whisk together the garlic, olive oil, and balsamic vinegar and pour the mixture over the mushrooms. Bake in a preheated 400 degree oven for 15 to 20 minutes.

Meanwhile, to make the pesto, place the bell pepper over an open flame and roast until the skin blisters and burns. Turn the pepper around to burn all sides. Set aside for a few minutes to continue steaming.

Roast the tomato in a small dry skillet in a pre-heated 400 degree oven for 10 minutes or until the skin starts to brown. (You could do this at the same time you bake the mushrooms.)

Peel the bell pepper and the tomato. Place them and all the remaining ingredients in a blender or food processor and mix until a pesto forms.

Spoon the pesto over the portobellos and watch your crowd of picky eaters rejoice!

SPAGHETTI SQUASH
WITH CRANBERRIES
AND ALMONDS

Makes 4 servings

1 spaghetti squash, cut
   in half lengthwise
⅓ cup olive oil
Juice of one lemon
1 cup dried cranberries
1 cup sliced skin-on
   almonds, toasted
½ cup chopped flat-leaf
   parsley

I love the vibrant yellow color of the spaghetti squash. Plus it is super easy to make, and lasts for several days after preparation.

Place the squash cut-side down on a lightly greased sheet pan. Pour one inch of water on the pan and cover with foil. Or use a baking pan with a cover if you have that.

Bake in a preheated 400 degree oven for about 30 minutes, or until it is soft when pierced with a fork. Remove, and turn the squash right side up. Using a fork, scrape the flesh to resemble spaghetti strands, and move into a bowl.

Season to taste with salt, then stir in the olive oil, lemon juice, and remaining ingredients.

Serve at room temperature.

FROM THE HEN HOUSE

We have, give or take, about 36 furry-footed hens on an average day. Coyotes are a major problem in Malibu, and because our birds free range on the property, some—sad to say—become a coyote's dinner every now and then.

Although we have lots of chickens, we don't usually eat our own, except that one time when we ate one of our roosters. And when I say "we," I mean my husband, John, who wanted to take the concept of self-sustaining all the way. If we eat chicken, he said, we have to have the guts to eat our own, or we should not be eating it at all. True, of course, in theory. But killing, plucking, and prepping a bird from your own flock is not for the faint of heart.

At the time we had forty chickens, twelve of which were very aggressive roosters who attacked anyone who approached the house. Because our chickens live in the front yard (where they are less likely to become coyote dinner) this proved to be a problem. After the mail carrier stopped delivering mail we knew we had to do something, and the initial solution was to eat them.

After cooking up one scrawny rooster, nobody wanted to do it ever again. So we placed an ad on Craigslist for free roosters. And they were gone.

The best advice I can give about cooking chicken is to buy organic, free-range, fresh chickens with no water or any other flavors injected into them.

CHICKEN + MUSTARD AND BREAD CRUMBS

THREE WAYS

Makes 6 servings

Mustard chicken #1:
6 tablespoons Dijon
    mustard
4 eggs
6 thin-pounded skinless
    chicken breasts,
    seasoned lightly with
    salt
1 cup flour
Butter and olive oil

Coating options:
30/30/30 mixture of dry
    bread crumbs, Parmesan
    cheese, and yellow
    cornmeal
Uncooked couscous
    (yes, you can coat your
    chicken with couscous—
    very crunchy and nice)

Chicken goes really well with mustard, and there are several ways to make a chicken-and-mustard dish. Following are three great and easy ways; they are all variations of the same recipe. Learn one and you will master three.

My "rule of crumb" is: The thinner the chicken, the finer the bread crumbs should be. So a thin breast goes well with dry bread crumbs, Parmesan cheese, and cornmeal or with couscous. A thicker, skin-on breast goes well with fresh bread crumbs or panko bread crumbs.

Combine the mustard and eggs. Dip the chicken in the flour. Then dip the chicken into the mustard-and-egg mixture. Finally, dip the chicken into your coating of choice (see left).

The chicken can be prepared to this stage and refrigerated one day in advance.

When ready to serve, sauté the breasts in butter and olive oil, two or three at a time maximum. Do not crowd your skillet. Sauté until brown and crispy (about 3 minutes per side). Transfer to paper towels to drain.

recipe continues

Mustard chicken #2:

6 skin-on chicken
    breasts, seasoned
    lightly with salt
Olive oil
6 tablespoons mustard
4 eggs

Coating options:

2 cups fresh bread
    crumbs, combined with
    3 tablespoons parsley
    and 1 tablespoon butter
Panko bread crumbs,
    whirled with parsley
    and a little olive oil
    in a food processor

First, sear the skin side of the chicken breasts in olive oil in a medium-hot skillet until the skin is brown and crisp (about 3 minutes). Remove from the skillet and allow to cool. The breast will still be raw inside.

Whisk together the mustard and eggs, and dip the seared, cooled chicken breast into the mixture. Then dip the chicken into your coating of choice; see left.

The chicken can be prepared to this stage one day in advance.

When ready to serve, bake the chicken in a preheated 375 degree oven for about 20 minutes, depending on the thickness, or until cooked through and the bread crumbs are brown and crispy.

Mustard chicken #3:

3/4 cup Dijon mustard
1 lemon, juiced
3 tablespoons olive oil
1 tablespoon fine-chopped
    fresh rosemary
Hot red chili flakes to
    taste
6 skin-on chicken
    breasts, seasoned
    lightly with salt
1 small bunch arugula

Mustard-fennel slaw:

2 fennel bulbs, sliced
    thin on the mandoline
    and seasoned with salt
3 tablespoons whole-
    grain mustard
1 lemon, juiced
1 teaspoon fine-chopped
    fresh rosemary
3 tablespoons olive oil

To make the marinade, combine all ingredients except the chicken and arugula in a bowl. Then dip and coat the chicken in the marinade. Return to the fridge and marinate overnight.

Toss all the slaw ingredients together.

When ready to serve, cook the chicken over a hot grill until done. If your chicken breasts are thick, it is best to partially grill them and then finish in the oven.

To serve, combine the mustard-fennel slaw with arugula and add the chicken.

MAMA TRAN'S VIETNAMESE CHICKEN SALAD

Makes 4 servings

For salad:
2 cups cooked chicken, shredded
1 cup cooked red quinoa
1 cup finely shredded cabbage
1 cup finely sliced cucumber, carrot, and cilantro
2 tablespoons black sesame seeds

Spicy sweet Asian dressing:
2 limes, juiced
2 garlic cloves, grated
5 tablespoons maple syrup
6 tablespoons fish sauce
1 tablespoon sriracha
½ cup water
¼ cup canola oil

I often teach cooking classes, but every once in a while, I get to *take* one. Ho Luong Tran, the mother of my friend Bic Tran, taught an informal class on Vietnamese cooking, and for once, I was the student.

I love Vietnam. I took my children there when they were young, and I hope to get back there one day. In the meantime, Mama Tran brought a little bit of Vietnam to me.

At the café, we make a version of the salad she taught me, with some minor changes. We serve it in little Chinese to-go containers with chopsticks at parties.

Combine the salad ingredients in a bowl.

Whisk together the dressing ingredients, pour over the salad, and toss.

CHICKEN, RICOTTA, AND BACON BURGER

Makes 4 large burgers
    or 8 sliders

For burgers:

1 pound boneless,
    skinless chicken
    breast, chopped

4 slices good bacon,
    minced fine

3/4 cup fresh ricotta
    cheese

Juice and some zest from
    1 lemon

1/2 cup chopped parsley

1/4 cup chopped red onion

1/4 cup grated Parmesan
    cheese

1/4 teaspoon salt

Brioche burger buns

For spicy aioli:

1/2 cup mayonnaise

2 tablespoons (or to
    taste) hot sauce of
    your choice, such as
    sriracha or chipotle
    peppers in adobo sauce

For garnish:

Arugula

Sliced tomatoes

Sliced red onion

This chicken burger is total killer. Including a little (or a lot of) bacon in the mixture makes it super juicy, and so does the ricotta cheese. We serve it both full size and as little sliders for appetizers. I prefer it with a spicy aioli, but you can also do a lemon aioli (p. 28).

Add all burger ingredients (except the buns, of course) to food processor. Pulse until properly blended. Do not overblend. Form with your hands into 4 large or 8 slider-size burgers.

Sauté or grill for a few minutes on each side or until browned and cooked through.

Mix together the mayo and hot sauce to make the aioli.

To assemble, toast the buns, spread 1/2 tablespoon aioli on the bun, add arugula, and then top with the burger. Place another 1/2 tablespoon aioli directly on the burger, and then top with sliced tomatoes and sliced red onion.

Tip: The burger patties freeze well, so you can make a large batch ahead of time.

CHICKEN + BROCCOLI
QUESADILLA

Makes 2 regular-size
   quesadillas or
   14 mini-quesadillas

½ pound cooked chicken
   breast, chopped fine
¾ pound cubed jalapeño
   Monterey Jack cheese
½ cup quick-cooked
   broccoli florets
½ cup chopped cilantro
2 green onions, cut thin
2 Roma tomatoes, seeded
   and cut fine
Whole wheat or regular
   tortillas, cut into
   mini-rounds or left
   whole
Spicy aioli (p. 242)

This is a great quesadilla, which we serve both as appetizer mini-quesadillas and as regular-size ones.

In a food processor, pulse the chicken, cheese, and broccoli until they just combine, but not so long that they turn into a gooey mess. Move to a bowl, and stir in the cilantro, green onions, and tomatoes.

Place the filling inside the tortillas, whichever size you are using.

If you are making mini-quesadillas, sauté to order. For regular-size, grill until the tortilla is a crispy brown and the cheese is melted. Serve with a dollop of spicy aioli on top.

Tip: These can be assembled ahead and frozen before sautéing or grilling.

CHICKEN +

CHERRY TOMATOES

Makes 6 servings

6 skin-on chicken breasts
  or thighs, lightly
  seasoned with salt

1 tablespoon butter

1 tablespoon olive oil

½ large onion, sliced
  thin

3 tablespoons crème
  fraîche

1 basket cherry tomatoes

½ cup pitted black olives

1 bunch thin green beans
  or asparagus

3 tablespoons roughly
  chopped parsley

Crème fraîche is great in any sauce for its slightly tangy taste. (For example, it's in the super thin turkey gravy, p. 255.) In cold dishes, sour cream can be substituted, but not in cooked dishes, as the sour cream breaks when heated, so don't try that here.

Sear the chicken, skin down, in butter and olive oil, in a cast-iron or other ovenproof skillet until it is nice and crispy. Do not crowd your pan, because then it will steam instead. So please do only a few pieces at a time, and only do the skin side so that the fat renders properly. Remove the chicken to a platter. It is still raw inside at this point.

Now in the same pan, sauté the onion for a few minutes until it begins to brown but before it is caramelized. Season with salt. Stir in the crème fraîche, cherry tomatoes, and olives.

Then place the chicken on top, and put the whole thing into a preheated 400 degree oven for about 12 minutes or until the chicken is done, depending on the thickness. When is the chicken done? When it is no longer pink inside. And what else has happened? The juices from the chicken have mixed with the crème fraîche and the juices from the tomatoes. Yum-yum.

While the chicken is baking, cook the green beans or asparagus in salted water very briefly and drain. Toss the green beans into the pan once it is out of the oven.

Taste for salt. It may need a dash. Finish off the whole thing with chopped parsley.

20/20/20 CHICKEN

Makes 4 servings

1 whole roasting chicken
2 tablespoons salt

Roasting a chicken requires almost no work. We are not going to baste it in butter. Or spray it with oil. We are not going to stuff it with a lemon or with herbs. We are not going to truss it either. All we are going to do is dry it, salt it, and bake it.

However, we are going to buy the best chicken we can find. Look for an organic, free-range chicken, the freshest bird you can find. Freezing chickens changes the texture so much that I don't recommend using a frozen chicken when roasting whole. The fresher the bird, the better the final result.

Dry and salt your chicken well all over, and place it, uncovered, in the refrigerator until ready to bake, 4 to 6 hours. Leaving the chicken uncovered will dry the skin, and the dryer the skin, the more crisp it will be. Yummy!

Bring the bird to room temperature before starting to roast it.

Either in a preheated cast-iron skillet or on a piece of parchment on a sheet pan, place the bird into a preheated 450 degree oven. Both methods will reduce the chances of the bird sticking to the pan.

And now apply the 20/20/20 rule: 20 minutes breast up, flip it over; 20 minutes breast down, flip it over; 20 minutes breast up. Done.

THANKSGIVING TURKEY

Makes 8 to 10 servings

1 medium (12-pound)
    turkey
2 cups chopped carrots,
    celery, and onion
1 stick butter
Olive oil spray

I love Thanksgiving. I love the big table and the look of a huge turkey. But even though big birds may look great, smaller turkeys cook much faster and are much tastier. So I always recommend a smaller turkey, rather than the big, impressive one. Your guests will be more impressed with the taste—I promise.

Three days in advance, rinse and dry the turkey thoroughly. Season well, inside and out, with salt and pepper. Return it to the refrigerator. You are now dry brining your turkey, which is a lot easier than doing a wet brine.

One day in advance (or on the day of the event), lightly sauté chopped vegetables in 1 stick of butter for a few minutes or until slightly translucent. Season with salt and pepper and allow to cool. The vegetables do not need to be cooked through.

Blot the turkey with paper towels to ensure it is nice and dry. Lightly spray with olive oil spray, lay cheesecloth over the breast, and place the 2 cups of cooked vegetables directly on top of the breast. This will prevent the breast from cooking too fast.

On the day of the event, if you're not there already, place your veggie-covered turkey in a preheated 450 degree oven for 45 minutes. Then reduce the oven temperature to 375 degrees until your turkey is done (about 2 hours more, depending on the size of your bird). Remove the veggie blanket at least 1 hour before the turkey is done to allow the turkey to brown all over. The vegetables can then be discarded. They have done their job—keeping the breast moist and keeping it from overcooking before the legs are cooked through.

Let the turkey rest before carving and serving with Super Thin Turkey Gravy (p. 255) on the side.

TURKEY BREAST STUFFED
WITH LEEKS

Some years my husband has been out of town for Thanksgiving, and it has been just the kids and me, one of whom is vegan. So cooking a whole turkey doesn't make a lot of sense. I love the simplicity and the quickness of cooking a turkey breast instead. The only challenge is getting it butterflied, which you can ask your butcher to do.

If your butcher can't accommodate you, just pound away. Cut it three-quarters of the way through to split it open in half and make it half as thick as it was originally. Then place it between plastic wrap and pound it a little more.

Your technique does not have to be pretty—you just need a reasonably thin turkey breast so you can roll it up.

Makes 4 to 6 servings

2 leeks, rinsed and
  sliced
2 garlic cloves, thinly
  sliced
2 tablespoons butter
½ cup chopped parsley
2 cups fresh bread crumbs
1 whole or half skin-
  on turkey breast,
  butterflied or flattened
  and rolled, lightly
  seasoned with salt
Olive oil

Sauté the leeks and the garlic in the butter on low heat until translucent. Stir in the parsley and the fresh bread crumbs, and cook for another minute or until the crumbs are slightly toasted. Season lightly with salt.

Place the turkey with the skin side down on a piece of plastic wrap, skin side on the far end (facing away from you). Spread the bread crumb mixture over the turkey, and then start to roll it up as tightly as you can, ending with the turkey skin covering the exterior portion of the roll. Tie it with kitchen string to make sure it holds together. Remove the plastic wrap.

Sear the turkey breast roll on all sides in olive oil, browning and crisping the skin for a few minutes. The roll can be made in advance up to this point and kept in the fridge until needed.

When ready to serve, place it in a preheated 375 degree oven for 30 to 40 minutes or until it reaches an internal temperature of 170 degrees. Let it rest for 5 minutes, and then slice it really thin and serve with Super Thin Turkey Gravy (p. 255).

SUPER THIN
TURKEY GRAVY

Makes 3 cups

2 cups sliced button
   mushrooms
2 tablespoons olive oil
1 tablespoon minced
   shallot
3 cups turkey stock
   (homemade or
   purchased)
½ lemon, juiced
3 tablespoons crème
   fraîche
1 tablespoon pink
   peppercorns
2 tablespoons chopped
   chives
Turkey drippings
   (optional)

I seldom use sauces and am not a huge gravy fan. But for Thanksgiving, I usually make this super thin (no thickener) gravy, which will work with either the stuffed turkey breast roll (p. 253) or a traditional whole turkey (p. 250).

In a large, heated skillet, cook the mushrooms in the olive oil for about 3 minutes or until just beginning to brown. Add shallot. Season lightly with salt and add the stock. Bring to a boil, then reduce to a simmer and cook for 5 minutes. Add lemon juice. Whisk in the crème fraîche, pink peppercorns, and chives. If available, whisk in the turkey drippings.

Tip: This gravy can be made one day in advance.

FROM THE VINEYARD

We have a small vineyard of 300 vines on our property, which we planted in 2008, with a mixture of Malbec and Carmenere grapes. I have yet to make wine, but the grapes are very drought tolerant and look amazing. And although they are wine grapes, they are super sweet and delicious to eat as is. But one day I will make wine!

In preparing my Malibu farm dinners, I have worked with local Malibu vineyards, and my first wine partner was Sonja Magdevski (p. 258) from Casa Dumetz Wines. She has a gorgeous Pinot Noir vineyard right around the corner from me, and she also has additional grapes growing on the Central Coast. Sonja is a great writer, an awesome winemaker, and a beautiful woman. She has a charming tasting room in Los Alamos, California, a few hours up the coast from Malibu.

In this chapter we are including recipes that are based on vinegar, also a product from the vineyard, as well as some wine-based drinks, including sangria. Mmm.

WINE-BASED DRINKS

THREE WAYS

Each makes 8 to 10
  servings

Strawberry basil
  sangria:
½ cup simple syrup
1 pound strawberries,
  quartered
2 oranges, sliced
3 bottles wine, red or
  rosé
½ cup brandy
½ cup triple sec
1 bunch basil leaves

Thyme nectarine sangria:
½ cup simple syrup
½ cup brandy
1½ cups sliced
  nectarines
3 bottles white wine
1 small bunch of thyme

Pineapple jalapeño sake
  cocktail:
½ cup simple syrup (1:1
  sugar/water ratio)
32 ounces pineapple juice
5 jalapeño chili peppers,
  thinly sliced
12 cups sake or tequila

At the café we serve a lot of sangria, which is a fun and easy way to serve wine with fruits. As it is served over ice, it is very refreshing on a hot summer day. Pick your poison—these are all delish!

No matter which of these you're making, the steps are the same. And they're easy, too. Combine all the ingredients, and allow to sit for 24 hours before serving over ice.

CHICKEN WITH BALSAMIC FIG VINEGAR REDUCTION

Makes 6 servings

6 boneless chicken
  breasts, skin-on,
  lightly seasoned
  with salt
4 tablespoons butter
2 tablespoons olive oil
1 red onion, sliced
⅓ cup balsamic fig
  vinegar (regular
  balsamic vinegar is OK
  as a substitute)
1 cup chicken stock
3 tablespoons chopped
  parsley
8 black Mission figs,
  sliced in half and
  seared until brown on
  the cut side (optional)

This is a really great, fast, and easy recipe and does not require that you marinate the chicken. Make it any night of the week.

Sear the chicken in 1 tablespoon butter and 1 tablespoon olive oil until the skin is crispy. Then finish it off in a preheated 375 degree oven until cooked through, about 10 to 12 minutes, depending on the thickness of the breasts. Remove the chicken to a plate and set aside.

In the same skillet, cook the red onion in a little more olive oil until beginning to soften. Season the onion with salt, pour in the fig vinegar, and let it reduce for a few minutes—but don't get carried away; we want the vinegar liquid still there. Then pour in 1 cup of chicken stock. Take the skillet off the heat, and whisk in the remaining 3 tablespoons butter.

Either keep the chicken breasts whole or slice them. Then pour the sauce on, over, or around the chicken. Sprinkle with parsley. If you like, top with the seared figs.

Fig-elicious!

LITTLE GEM LETTUCE

+ CANDY CANE BEET

Makes 4 servings

For salad:
1 large candy cane beet
2 heads little gem
   lettuce
Toasted sunflower seeds
   (optional)

For chop dressing:
2 tablespoons Dijon
   mustard
Sprinkle of salt
1 teaspoon finely chopped
   shallot
2 tablespoons red wine
   vinegar
½ cup vegetable oil

Sometimes the very best thing is the simplest thing: a bowl full of little gem lettuce with thinly sliced beets.

Slice the beet on a mandoline into a bowl of ice water. The slices will curl and be nice and crunchy.

While they soak a little, make the dressing. Whisk together the mustard, salt, shallot, and red wine vinegar. You are looking for a texture that is thinner than cream but thicker than water. Then whisk in the vegetable oil in a slow stream. The dressing will last several days in the fridge.

When ready to serve, toss the dressing with the lettuce, taste for salt, and top with sliced beet. If desired, top with toasted sunflower seeds.

RED BEET QUINOA

2 cups quinoa, cooked
2 red beets, skin on
Olive oil
Dash of sugar
¼ cup red wine vinegar
¼ cup fresh lemon juice
½ shallot, finely chopped
Herbs, for garnish

I usually have beets in my vegetable beds year round. I love how they are so easy to grow and can stay in the soil for weeks or even months before getting too old to use. In this way, beets are unlike some crops, such as green beans, which need picking every day.

Mixing quinoa with marinated beets gives the quinoa a gorgeous color, and quinoa absorbs the beets in perfect harmony.

Drizzle the beets with olive oil and a splash of water. Place in a small ovenproof container, cover with foil, and roast in a preheated 400 degree oven until just soft when pierced, 1 hour. Allow to cool, then peel the skin of the beets by rubbing a paper towel over them or by rubbing them under running water. Chop them finely, season with salt and a tiny dash of sugar, and drizzle with more olive oil. Combine them in a bowl with vinegar, lemon juice, and shallot. Marinate for 30 minutes or overnight.

Pour beets into the cooked quinoa, and stir until well combined. Garnish with herbs—I prefer dill for this recipe, but you can add anything you like, such as parsley or cilantro.

RAW CHARD SALAD WITH CRANBERRIES + PEPITAS

Makes 4 to 6 servings

1 bunch chard
Pinch of sugar
Drizzle of good olive oil
Splash of balsamic
  vinegar
Dried cranberries, figs,
  or sliced grapes
Sweetened pepitas: sauté
  2 cups raw pepitas with
  1/3 cup agave or honey
  and 2 tablespoons olive
  oil for a few minutes,
  stirring frequently.
  Once the seeds begin
  to brown, transfer to
  a greased sheet pan to
  cool. Sprinkle with
  salt and chop into
  pieces.

Chard grows really well in Malibu, and I often have masses of it. I don't like cooked chard that much, but raw chard with a dried fruit I love.

Slice the chard into thin ribbons, and then gently massage the leaves with salt, pepper, sugar, and a little olive oil until they are nice and glossy. (If you don't massage it, it doesn't absorb any dressing. Then it's just raw chard tickling your throat, and really, who wants to eat that?)

Splash with balsamic vinegar, toss in dried fruit or grapes, and top with sweetened pepitas.

Tip: You can store the sweetened pepitas covered for one week at room temperature.

TRI-COLOR CHOPPED

SALAD WITH CRISPY

PANCETTA

Makes 4 to 6 servings

4 cups assorted lettuces, chopped, such as romaine, iceberg, radicchio, arugula

½ cup garbanzo beans

½ cup chopped tomatoes

¼ cup chop dressing (p. 264)—this salad is how it got its name!

½ cup shredded Cheddar cheese

8 ounces crispy pancetta or prosciutto either baked on a lightly greased sheet pan or sautéed in a skillet until just crispy

Chopped salad is such a classic dish—it has been around for a long time. I like to make mine very simple, using several different lettuces and, most important, crispy pancetta.

Toss together lettuces, garbanzo beans, and tomatoes with the dressing. Season with salt.

Stir in the cheese, and toss with the crispy pancetta.

Tip: At the café, we make a vegan chopped salad by substituting chopped, roasted butternut squash, chopped beets, and avocado for the cheese and prosciutto.

PURPLE KALE
+ PURPLE PLUMS

Makes 4 servings

1 bunch purple kale,
  sliced
Pinch of sugar
Drizzle of good olive oil
2 tablespoons
  pomegranate molasses
  or sour cherry syrup
2 tablespoons balsamic
  vinegar
1 cup thinly sliced
  purple plums or grapes
Sweetened pepitas (p. 268)
  or crumbled goat or
  blue cheese (optional)

Purple salad is stunning. There is no such thing as too much purple, and OK, we have established that tone-on-tone color combos are super cool, but seriously, what is cooler than purple on purple? Yeah, that's right—nothing.

Toss the purple kale with a little salt, a pinch of sugar, and a drizzle of olive oil, and massage the leaves for a few seconds. Then toss in the molasses and balsamic vinegar, and taste for salt.

Place on a platter, and top with the grapes and the pepitas or cheese (if using).

FROM
THE BAKER

and the pastry maker

I am not a big baker because baking requires exactness, and my cooking style is very much a little bit of that and a little bit of this. I do not believe that measuring is a necessity in cooking. Instead, I focus on tasting as I go—that is what dictates the recipe.

Baking, however, is a totally different beast: Precision is king and measurements rule. I don't mess with bread at all, but my friend Bob Oswaks makes great crunchy bread. He has a bakery, Bob's Well Bread Bakery, near Sonja Magdevski's tasting room for Casa Dumetz Wines in Los Alamos (pp. 257–259). He says:

> Good bread is about the simplest ingredients (flour, water, salt, and a leavening agent—yeast). I use organic flour, filtered or spring water, and French sea salt, and my yeast is a wild yeast levain starter. But through the process of fermentation, you get something magical, which transcends the simplicity of the ingredients.

All the Malibu Farm baking and pastry recipes are super easy—just mix and pour—and most of them have been reworked over the years to fit the style of our farm, with the original source recipe long lost. I very much like all my baking to be "home style," and I prefer that it not look too professional. To me, something that looks homemade always tastes better than something that looks perfect!

WHOLE WHEAT BERRY
CRUMBLE WITH AGAVE

Makes 4 to 6 servings

For crumb topping:
¾ cup whole wheat flour
½ cup walnuts
½ cup sugar
6 tablespoons butter, cut
  into small cubes

For berry mixture:
4 cups berries—
  strawberries, mixed
  berries, or anything
  you like
4 stalks rhubarb, cut
  thin (optional)
1 lemon, juiced
⅓ cup agave syrup
2 tablespoons flour

Whipped cream or powdered
  sugar (optional)

I have been making berry crumble my whole life. It's one of those desserts you never tire of. I make a large batch of the crumb mixture and keep it in the freezer. When we suddenly have guests, or if I feel like something sweet, all I need to do is toss some berries with a squeeze of lemon juice and agave, pull out the crumbs, scatter them on top, and bake until done. Can't get any easier than that!

Pulse the crumb topping ingredients in a food processor until coarsely combined. Do not overprocess.

If you are using strawberries, cut them in half. If you are using other berries, you can leave them whole. Toss the berries and rhubarb with the lemon, agave, and flour. Then place the mixture in a decorative ovenproof container or divide it among individual ramekins. Top with the crumb mixture, and bake in a preheated 375 degree oven for about 45 minutes or until the crumb mixture is a crispy brown and the berry mixture is bubbling and thickened.

Serve with whipped cream and/or powdered sugar if you like.

Tip: You can use frozen berries, but double the amount of flour in that case, as they release a lot of juice.

SALTED CARAMEL
ICE CREAM COOKIE
SANDWICHES

One day you're in and the next day you're out. Suddenly salted caramel butterscotch pudding was old news, and salted caramel ice cream was the new darling. Everyone was talking about it, and I wanted to try it. Badly. I Googled "salted ice cream," and then I made a few batches in my ice cream maker. Didn't love it. Tried it at a few trendy places, was not in love.

I didn't like the way the ice cream was flavored throughout with the salted caramel. Then I realized what I really wanted (needed, craved, hungered for) was a salted caramel ice cream cookie sandwich. I actually hate most ice cream sandwiches because they are too thick. I wanted something very thin and elegant—something I could eat without straining my jaw muscles too much. This recipe is it.

For salted caramel:
½ cup sugar
½ heaping teaspoon good
　salt

For cookies:
1 stick salted butter
½ cup sugar
⅓ cup brown sugar
1 egg
1 teaspoon vanilla
1 cup + 2 tablespoons
　flour
¼ teaspoon salt
½ teaspoon baking soda

To assemble:
1 pint vanilla ice cream

To make the salted caramel: First, melt the sugar in a dry, heavy-bottomed pan. Pay attention. Don't burn it, because burned caramel tastes pretty bad. If it begins to burn around the edges while the center is still not melted, then lift the pan away from the heat for a few seconds and swirl the sugar around. You want it melted and a uniform medium-dark caramel color. Take it just to the very edge of burning. If you burn it, start over. Don't taste or touch it. Caramel is hot and if you touch it, you are going to get hurt.

When you have reached the uniform medium-brown color, toss in the salt and pour the whole thing onto a sheet pan. Cool until hardened.

Bang it, hit it, break it into little pieces. Set aside.

To make the cookies: Beat together the butter and sugars until light and fluffy. Add egg and vanilla. You may need to scrape the bowl to get the mixture to blend properly.

In a small bowl, combine the flour, salt, and baking soda, and add to the butter mix. Blend until just incorporated. Blend lightly and quickly. Now fold in about one-third of the salted caramel pieces.

This cookie dough can be frozen until you are ready to bake.

These babies are going to really spread out to be super thin and will triple in size. So although it does not look like a lot of dough, resist the urge to fit everything onto one sheet pan. You are going to need two. Place 1 tablespoon dollops of cookie dough, evenly spaced, on two parchment-covered cookie sheets. The dough will make about 24 cookies. Bake in a 375 degree preheated oven for 12 minutes.

To assemble: Take the ice cream out of the freezer, let it soften for a few minutes, and then stir in the remaining salted caramel pieces. Return the ice cream to the freezer.

When your cookies are ready and cooled, spread a small amount of ice cream (or a large amount—it's your sandwich) between two.

Tip: To clean your pan or utensils after making caramel, just add really hot water, which will dissolve the stuck-on hardened sugar.

SAFFRON ICE CREAM

Makes 1 quart

1 teaspoon saffron

1 14-ounce can coconut
  milk

Same amount of whole-
  milk plain yogurt—use
  the empty coconut milk
  can for measurement
  (yeah, yeah, you could
  use nonfat, but nonfat
  yogurt is awful)

Same amount of sugar—
  again, use the empty
  coconut milk can for
  measurement

1 lemon, juiced

Crème fraîche whipped
  cream: Fold ½
  cup crème fraîche
  into 1 cup heavy
  cream whipped with
  1 tablespoon sugar
  until medium soft peaks
  form. Makes 1½ cups.

I don't make a lot of homemade ice creams,
but when I do, I like to use ingredients
and flavors not available in the market.

Saffron ice cream is super delicious but
sweet, so I prefer it with a dollop of crème
fraîche whipped cream.

To make the ice cream, dissolve the saffron into the coconut milk,
and heat for a few minutes until the coconut milk has turned a
lovely yellow. Let cool. Stir in the yogurt, sugar, and lemon juice.
Taste for seasoning. Add more lemon if needed.

Pour into ice cream maker, and churn per manufacturer's
instructions.

Serve with crème fraîche whipped cream on top.

BASIL ICE CREAM

Makes 1 quart

2 cups sugar

1 bunch fresh lemon basil
  (or regular basil)

1 8-ounce package cream
  cheese

1½ cups whole-milk plain
  yogurt

Zest of 1 lemon

1 tablespoon lemon juice

1 cup heavy cream,
  whipped

Berries (optional)

Basil ice cream is totally yummy. And a conversation starter. If you are going to go to the bother of making ice cream, make something you can't buy at an ice cream store. And please don't ever make lavender ice cream. That's awful—and so 1998.

In a food processor, whirl sugar with basil until incorporated. Add cream cheese, yogurt, lemon zest, and lemon juice. Blend until properly mixed, but don't get carried away.

Stir in the whipped cream. If you are so inclined, you can stir in some raspberries or other berries. (Or you might want to serve the berries on the side.)

Pour into ice cream maker, and churn per manufacturer's instructions.

Tip: Try this recipe with cilantro instead! Just substitute lime zest and juice for the lemon.

BAY LEAF–SCENTED
YOGURT CAKE

<u>Makes 6 to 8 servings</u>

6 small fresh bay leaves
Zest of 1 lemon
1 cup sugar
1 stick butter
1 teaspoon vanilla
2 eggs
1 cup yogurt
1½ cups flour
1 teaspoon baking powder
½ teaspoon baking soda

This cake is deliciously **tart from the yogurt. Make a simple icing by combining** 1 cup powdered sugar with **a few drops of** lemon juice until you reach the desired consistency. My **favorite garnish is passion fruit, which makes it super extra tart, but you can also serve the cake with whipped cream and berries. Here we garnished it with icing and pink currants.**

In a food processor, make your bay leaf–scented sugar by processing the bay leaves and lemon zest in the sugar until pulverized.

Cream the bay leaf–scented sugar with the butter and vanilla in a mixing bowl until soft and fluffy. Add the eggs and yogurt. Then sift in the remaining dry ingredients and combine.

Pour the batter into a buttered and floured cake pan, and bake in a preheated 375 degree oven for about 45 minutes or until a knife inserted comes out clean.

Tip: You can use bay leaf–scented sugar in any recipe that calls for sugar. Mmm.

BLACK SESAME SEED

PANNA COTTA

For panna cotta:
1 cup cream
¼ cup sugar
1 teaspoon gelatin,
   dissolved in
   4 tablespoons water
1 cup whole-milk plain
   yogurt
1 teaspoon vanilla

For black sesame seed
   sugar:
½ cup sugar
3 tablespoons black
   sesame seeds
½ lemon, juiced

Panna cotta is basically flan without eggs. You can make it with yogurt, cream, or buttermilk. I suppose you could also make it with milk, but I'm not sure why you would want to. Creamier is better. I also like mine super soft, but if you prefer a less yielding texture, just add more gelatin.

Place cream into a saucepan with the sugar, and cook on medium heat. Stir until the mixture comes to a light boil and the sugar is fully dissolved. Don't let it boil over!

Pour the mixture over the softened gelatin, and then pour the entire thing (cream and gelatin) back into the pot. Make sure all the gelatin has left the bowl and is now in the pot. Whisk so that the new mixture is properly blended. Now remove the mixture from the heat, and stir in the yogurt and the vanilla.

Pour immediately into molds or containers. If you plan to unmold your panna cotta, lightly oil the molds first.

To make the black sesame seed sugar, combine the sugar, sesame seeds, and lemon juice in a small saucepan, and cook over low heat until sugar is dissolved (about 2 minutes).

To serve, either unmold or don't, then drizzle with the black sesame seed sugar.

GRILLED CHOCOLATE CAKE + CARAMEL SAUCE

I prefer cakes that can be made way in advance and frozen. Olive oil cake (p. 225) freezes very well; so does crumb mixture (p. 276) and cookie dough (p. 279). I usually have an assortment of such frozen goods in my freezer, ready to be taken out for an unexpected guest or a last-minute catering job.

This chocolate cake also freezes very well and can be thrown directly on the grill from the freezer, so how easy is that?

Once it's grilled, drizzle it with brown sugar caramel, dust with salt, and top with whipped cream. Yum, yum.

recipe continues

For caramel sauce:
2 cups brown sugar
½ cup corn syrup
   (optional)
Touch of water
2 cups heavy cream
½ cup butter

For chocolate cake:
3½ cups flour
3½ cups sugar
1 cup unsweetened cocoa
   powder
1 teaspoon salt
3 teaspoons baking soda
1½ cups kefir
1½ cups canola oil
4 eggs

For grilling:
Powdered sugar

For garnish:
Whipped cream

To make the caramel sauce: Combine the brown sugar and the corn syrup with a touch of water in a heavy-bottomed skillet, and cook over low heat for about 12 minutes or until the sugar starts to reduce and thicken, and large bubbles form. If you prefer to not use corn syrup, you can omit it and add just the touch of water.

While the sugar is cooking, combine the cream and butter, and melt in the microwave or on the stovetop.

When the caramel is ready, pour in the cream-and-butter mixture and stir until combined. Set aside.

To make the cake: Combine the flour, sugar, cocoa powder, salt, and baking soda in a bowl. Combine the kefir, canola oil, and eggs in a separate bowl.

Now add the wet ingredients to the dry ingredients, and stir until well blended.

Pour into a buttered and floured 8- or 10-inch cake pan, and bake in a preheated 375 degree oven for 30 minutes or until just done. (Once cool, wrap and freeze if you're doing that.)

To grill, dust the cake with powdered sugar and grill on a barbecue.

To serve the cake, top it with brown sugar caramel sauce, salt, and whipped cream.

Tip: This recipe makes a lot of caramel sauce (4 to 5 cups), but it lasts for a few weeks in the fridge, so I make a large batch to keep. You can pop it in the microwave for a few seconds before serving, as it gets super thick when it is cold.

UPSIDE-DOWN CHERRY CORNMEAL GOODNESS CAKE

2 tablespoons butter

2 tablespoons agave syrup

2 tablespoons pomegranate molasses

5 cups pitted cherries

¾ cup flour

⅓ cup cornmeal

Pinch of salt

1½ teaspoons baking powder

1 stick salted butter

¾ cup sugar

2 eggs

1 teaspoon vanilla

⅓ cup buttermilk or kefir

Whipped cream or powdered sugar (optional)

Catch them while you can! California cherry season is short and sweet. This is a super easy and fast dessert, or a great breakfast bread on an indulgent spring morning.

In a small (8-inch) ovenproof skillet, melt the butter with the agave and pomegranate molasses. Add the cherries. When combined, set the cherry mixture aside.

In a small bowl, stir together flour, cornmeal, salt, and baking powder. Set aside.

In a mixer, combine the butter and sugar until light and fluffy (about 5 minutes). Add the eggs, one at a time, then the vanilla and buttermilk. Once you add the buttermilk, the wet mixture will curdle—not to worry. Add the dry mixture and mix just until combined. Do not overmix.

Pour this combined wet-and-dry mixture over the cherry mixture.

Bake the cake in a preheated 375 degree oven for about 35 minutes or until just baked through and a skewer inserted in the center comes out clean. Let cool for a few minutes, and then turn the cake upside down. Do not let the cake cool completely before releasing it from the skillet, as the cherry mixture will become too sticky to release. When the cake is still warm, it will come out more easily.

Serve with whipped cream or powdered sugar, if desired.

AFFOGATO

ICE CREAM WITH SHOT OF ESPRESSO

Makes 2 servings

4 scoops vanilla ice
  cream
2 shots espresso

Some very simple things are the very best things. A shot of espresso over vanilla ice cream—it does not get much simpler or better. At the café we use Caffe Luxxe coffee and a Santa Barbara–made vanilla ice cream.

If you do not have an espresso machine—and OK, who does?—you can make a strong cup of drip espresso with your regular coffee maker.

Divide the ice cream between two glasses. Add one shot of espresso to each. Watch two very content people enjoy!

THANK YOU

Many people have made the dream of Malibu Farm and this
book a reality.

First of all, I would like to thank my lovely mother,
Harriet Henderson. When she died, she left me a small
inheritance. Without it, I couldn't have opened the café.
I am so grateful to her.

I also need to acknowledge my motherland—your support has
been overwhelming and unbelievable. Every day, my café
is filled with Swedish visitors, a steady stream from the
homeland, who have heard from friends of friends that a
Swede has a café on the Malibu Pier, which they must visit.
You support me in droves. Sweden, you will always be the
center of my heart and the core of who I am.

And I extend my gratitude to my adopted home, the City
of Malibu, and the residents here. I did not start Malibu
Farm. Instead, Malibu grew it for me. Krishna Jaret, Megan
Bee, Netti Bode, Sasha Rondell, Kristen McCarron, Seth
Jaret, and Connie Hyman, you were the original crew, the
seed that started it all. And the residents of Malibu
have supported the café unwaveringly. I am the luckiest
transplant ever to arrive!

My wonderful husband, John Stockwell, was the one to
suggest that I pursue the pier location. I did not believe
that a restaurant of mine could survive there. So here
goes, John: You were right. Thank you!

Alexander Leff and the Malibu Pier partners, you took a chance on a small, local business owner with no previous restaurant experience, and I am so happy that you did.

Vanessa Alexander, you are a genius! Only one person could have done what you did with the restaurant design guidelines you had. With a shoestring budget, you created magic. Many thanks.

Netti Bode and Patrick Jensen, you have my heartfelt appreciation for creating the Malibu Farm logo.

Artimal Books, led by Martin Löf: Your photos and passion for the project made this book happen. And I owe a debt of gratitude to Patrick Leo of Artimal Books for the layout and design.

Kathy Keiser of editcetera: Thank you for your editing assistance of the first printing of this book. Without it, the recipes would be less than precise!

Thank you Amanda Englander, the determined, enthusiastic force of nature that made the second edition and full market release a reality. Thanks, too, to the rest of the Clarkson Potter team: Anna Mintz, Lauren Velasquez, Marysarah Quinn, Sonia Persad, Amy Boorstein, Mark McCauslin, and Philip Leung.

Last but not least, I acknowledge Arnold, Casey, Quincy, Hopper, Stanley, Fennel, Cloud, the twenty-three chickens, the queen bee, and the worker bees, the creatures who make the farm Malibu Farm.